Dedication
To my mum, niece and Nephew

AUTHOR'S WORDS

I thank everyone that has contributed immensely to the success of this book. Your contribution made this book possible and without you, I must acknowledge that it may not be possible. I also appreciate all the entrepreneurs and professionals that I used their stories and those I borrowed from their wealth of experiences. Thank you very much.

Finally to Almighty God, I give you all the glory.

FOREWORD
By Jonathan O. Oyibo, PMP

Would you like to have some tips for building a successful business or successful organization? If you have dreams of building a high performance and enduring organization, then, you may not want to miss reading this comprehensive guide that has been put together for such purpose.

This guide is written from the vast and vibrant consultancy experiences of the author, combined with experiences of other successful operators. As you read, you will be completely immersed into the sea of general knowledge of ideas generation, evaluation and brilliant implementation for successful and enduring businesses. It encompasses majority of the processes for building amazingly successful organization.

Even though, this guide does not present entirely new theories, it does offer great insight into the complex but interesting situation of ideas generation, evaluation and implementation, hence, deeply unveils the secret to success of several successful organizations around the world. It could be a good guide against early closure of Micro, Small and Medium Scale Enterprises (MSMEs), if meticulously deployed. This could also be a revolutionary insight that needs to be applied.

It provides an in-depth explanation on how to create economically profitable ideas; it contains necessary materials, templates and tools that can be applied to give extended lease of life to MSMEs

As good oil is for the working of a mechanical engine, so is creativity and innovation in the business arena. Without creativity and innovation thoroughly under-pinned by new ideas generation, organizations' continuity in (competitive) businesses will always shortly run out of steam.

The book contains eight chapters, each giving a brilliant explanation of the different parts of the creative process of Ideas.

Each chapter starts interestingly with a wisdom quote, most relevant to the topic, and calls to a learning action and realization for the reader. Besides the generous details therein, each chapter also closes with a summary of key points of the essential content of the chapter, making the book an easy-to-read piece.

The intelligible **templates and tools** used to demonstrate each of the processes explained in each chapter portray the efforts tactfully harnessed to make this a comprehensive guide.

Let me write briefly about the interesting bits of each of the chapters.

Chapter one expansively explains the origin of the **Suggestion Box** and dramatically unveils its usefulness as a powerful tool for ideas generation. Ironically, most organizations don't take the outcome from their suggestion boxes seriously. After reading this guide, you might consider becoming an advocate for the age-long tradition of Suggestion Box. A great deal of the value of the organization lies in the ears of the workers; the key to success is embracing the culture of listening to and understanding what lies in their hearts. In this chapter, the author explains how management often reacts to new ideas, and how you can avoid several of these common pit-falls which have been embedded in the plethora of this book.

Chapter two explains the processes for **Generating Business Ideas**. It unveils how you can distinguish great ideas lurking around you, from challenges, frustration, pain-points and opportunities. There are several techniques and strategies for generating business ideas. This chapter has listed and explained several of these techniques and strategies. It is very essential to know 'Pain-Points' are the catalysts for great business ideas. Template and tools are included in the book to show you how to hunt for your pain-points.

Chapter three deals with how you can **evaluate** your business ideas easily and quickly. Your evaluation will show how well these ideas will be acceptable. It gives you the opportunity to put your ideas to test before implementation. The various steps for evaluating ideas are well explained with the necessary template and tools in this chapter.

Generating new business ideas is an iterative process that progressively elaborates into a valuable product or service.

Your idea is worth nothing on paper; it has to be moved from notion to reality. Chapter four explains how this can be done and identifies how brilliant execution of your ideas can become the key to your business success. The **implementation of the ideas** must be true to the proposed vision.

This chapter also explains how to make the right decision during the implementation stage of a good idea. Explicit case studies are also used to clarify this chapter.

Chapter five encourages you to assess your strength and weakness; note the tangible and intangible skills. The chapter offers a unique and comprehensive **Personal Strength and Weakness Assessment (PSWA)** checklist and template. This tool will help you identify what you can be best or world-class at. The chapter also explains how building a culture of learning and creating a learning organization can be a big win.

Chapter six explains how **Creativity and Business** can be close partners and how you can create a **unique business formula** and build an enduring value system for your business.

Chapter seven explains the **Marketing of Product** of your Business Ideas. The importance of choosing the right customers is well emphasized and the enterprise should be built around the various needs of customers.

Lastly, the eighth chapter deals with the **Route to Success** by pulling together all the elements of the previous chapters in order to build a realistic plan for success. This plan becomes your Business Strategy. The Business Plan should answer all the questions from prospective investors or partners.

On a final note, I recommend **Idea Factory** as a reference guide for start-up businesses and on-going concerns that may want to add fresh lease of live to their businesses. Business Schools will also find this guide very useful for their students especially on Enterprise Management Studies and Programmes.

Many thanks to Mr. Tomisin Ajiboye for putting this valuable guide together for the benefit of seekers of successful business knowledge.

Table of Contents

Foreword ....

Introduction..

Suggestion Box...

Generating Business Ideas..

Evaluating Business Ideas ....

Implementing Business Ideas ....

You and your Ideas ....

Business and Ideas ....

Marketing your Product/Services ....

Route to Success ....

About the Author...

Introduction

There is nothing as powerful as an idea whose time has come ~ anonymous.

This book is intended to be both inspiring and practical, to offer some great ideas for building creative businesses, but at the same time warns that it's not easy. It is for start-ups and established enterprises, large and small. It aims to be readable as a whole and also useful for quick reference, section by section.

Most of what I have written in the following pages were learnt from my own experiences and those of others. My best qualifications are not my academic and professional ones but those gained from having been 'there', done it, got it wrong and then sometimes got it right. I have been involved in running workers' cooperatives, social enterprises and businesses in the creative sector even before the term 'creative industries' was invented. I've dealt with all the issues in this book meticulously and I am still learning.

The Creative Industries are hugely important to Nigeria's economy in these difficult times and they are going to become more important in the future.

If the future is going to be bright for our Creative Industries, we need our small and medium scale businesses to have rich and useful business ideas, sound business skills and a strong entrepreneurial base. That's an essential driver of growth and prosperity in a modern economy.

At this point in time, the average life span of an SME in Nigeria is about 24 months. It's at that point a poorly conceived business idea begins to show its deficiencies.

How can we stop that from happening? How can we prolong the life expectancy of a creative business and turn it into the success it sets out to be? This is something that I have written about in this book:

exploring rich ideas through creative tools to improve and revolutionize our business strategies.

I have established in each chapter a working theme and basis for understanding the usefulness of continuously generating, evaluating and implementing ideas in business. Creativity and business skills don't always go hand in hand – but both are needed to succeed in the 21st century. There are two schools of thought that there are left sided brains and right sided brains and never shall the duo meet; or, that those working in the creative and cultural fields just don't do business because they've never had the training and support to do so. What this dilemma demonstrates is that there is a management skills' gap and we need to address this.

This book approaches the management skills that bring together creative thinking and business skills. Idea Factory provides examples of how creative and business brains can merge to give birth to successful enterprises through idea management system. The book illustrates how the best business ideas and concepts can be used in the context of creative enterprises.

I have used my knowledge and experience to articulate and illustrate essential business strategies in a way that is appealing to creative entrepreneurs. As such, **Idea Factory** makes an important contribution to the management skills of creative entrepreneurs and consequently to the success of their enterprises or organizations.

My approach to consultancy and training is not to lecture but to facilitate – to offer some thoughts and experience to stimulate new ideas and empower others – then help people to find the individual solutions that suit their enterprise. It is in the same spirit that I have written this book. As you read this guide, bear in mind that nothing in it is absolute. Each idea needs to be adapted to your own circumstances and ethos; each is offered as a starting point rather than a conclusion. If it prompts you to find a more effective solution, that's fine.

The purpose of this book is not to tell you how to run your business but simply to provide some ideas and support.

My inspiration comes from the hundreds of people I have worked with and advised in my Industries over the years.

The Creative Industries turn creative talents into income streams for the owners of the intellectual property that this talent creates. Britain is now a leader in the Creative Industries and that's why the British Government is supporting this growing economy. Britain has a lot to offer the rest of the world and the British Council is promoting the ideas of the creative industries worldwide. UNESCO is also supporting the Cultural Industries in the developing world.

Some of my most recent works are on the internet and Creative Africa Network (CAN) which supports a wide range of creative enterprises, both established and new. This book builds on the success of those works. Several of the points made in this guide are illustrated by examples of CAN businesses, but the themes are universal and I have also drawn on my work with other organizations as well as my international experience of consultancy and training.

My idea is to intimate you of where we are coming from and take you on that smooth ride to a destination you may never look back from again. I am positive that after you finish and successfully apply the techniques from this book, you would realize you've laid your hands on a gold mine.

1
Suggestion Box Idea

- This chapter will help you appreciate the usefulness of your suggestion box and how well it served many organisations.

- It will reveal to you how suggestions could have helped the growth of many organizations if they had been properly managed.

- Why it suddenly faded out.

"Companies or individuals looking to replace an aging suggestion box should carefully consider moving straight to idea management, avoiding the inevitable problems of the suggestion box and increasing the likelihood of successful projects." - Mark Turrell

The concepts of Idea Management System (IMS) are partly founded on the original approach of the suggestion box. Idea management builds on the hundred-year old principles of the simple idea box, and adds collaboration, business focus, and a structured review and workflow process to ensure that the idea generation and development process is closely aligned with current and future business needs.

This chapter will explore the history of the suggestion box, the drawbacks of the traditional approach, and compare the suggestion box to the more sophisticated IMS approach.

THE HISTORY OF SUGGESTION BOX

The first recorded suggestion program was implemented in 1770 by the British Navy. They realized the need for a process for listening to every individual in the organization - without fear of reprisal. At that time, the mere mention of an idea that contradicted a captain or admiral's opinion was likely to be punished by hanging.

The first physical box to collect ideas appeared at William Denny & Brothers shipyard in Scotland in 1880. It was intended to collect ideas from all employees and pay a 'fair' reward for each implementable idea. This approach of the suggestion scheme, as it is still known in the United Kingdom today, spread rapidly through the country following government reports on the project's success.

In 1892 National Capital Region (NCR) became the first US Company to implement a company-wide suggestion program. The concept was the 'hundred-headed brain', developed by John Patterson, their infamous CEO. He realized early in his business career that employees had valuable ideas but that management structures tended to prevent these ideas from spreading through the company. Employees complained that there was no point giving ideas to their supervisors as the best ideas were stolen, and the worst ideas were used as a pretext for their dismissal.

Suggestion boxes became popular in the manufacturing sector over the years. They became part of the total quality movement and an integral part of cost, safety and quality improvement initiatives over the following fifty years. They were adopted by every other part of the world and they are still the mainstay of corporate suggestion programs, be they physical boxes or virtual boxes.

I first ran into a suggestion box many years back. It was in my church and it was love at first sight. I wanted to explore it, handle it, caress it, hug it, kiss it; I wanted it to be everything at that moment. I started by dropping every idea that came to mind every week till I got called up by my youth director to take charge and handle the suggestion box. That day was the beginning of my life.

WHAT BECAME OF OUR SUGGESTION BOX?

Have you ever considered what the single most important factor underlying the success of many thriving businesses might be? Is it our free enterprise system, superior management, or people with a willingness to work hard? I would argue that while all of these factors have contributed to our business success, none of them qualify as being singularly most important. In my opinion, *the success of thriving businesses is mostly dependent on the rapid acceptance of new ideas*, i.e. the unique ability to foster, accept, and apply those ideas which evolve from the minds of men. After all, without the development and eventual use of new ideas, progress would be nonexistent.

". He explained that while manufacturers in this country had many ideas for improving their operations, there existed no system for soliciting those ideas, testing them, and implementing those, which appeared promising."

Few years ago, I was traveling through the industrial districts, which surround Ikeja, Lagos. While visiting with the manager of a plant which manufactures female hair products, he spoke of his firm's difficulty maintaining its competitive position with other Nigerian manufacturers. There were many factors such as available financing, trade restrictions, corporate taxes and logistics, which the manager claimed were contributing to his firm's competitive disadvantage. However, near the end of our discussion, the manager became more philosophical in his lamentations. Eventually, he admitted that those factors mentioned as being competitive burdens on his firm were actually only the end products of a more basic dilemma. The manager finally acknowledged that Nigerian industrialists had long ago lost the battle of the suggestion box. He explained that while manufacturers in this country had many ideas for improving their operations, there existed no system for soliciting those ideas, testing them, and implementing those which appeared promising.

A New Idea

Obviously not all new ideas contribute to the success of a business. It has been said that of every one hundred ideas generated in the minds of men, only one will ultimately be expressed as a suggestion. Perhaps, only one out of every ten suggestions will be given serious consideration by management. Furthermore, not all of those suggestions considered will be tested, and only a small proportion of those tested will prove worthy of application. The odds, therefore, are about 100,000 to 1 that a mentally generated idea will ultimately prove useful. The relevant question is: can you take a risk of missing out on that one idea?

What became of your suggestion box? Have you ever used one? Does there exist in your firm a system that encourages the expression of new ideas? Unfortunately, it is relatively easy for a manager to squelch a new idea, but much more difficult to solicit, consider and test it. Some managers are totally unaware that they have become practicing "idea killers". These managers believe that they remain open-minded about suggestions for improvement, but unbeknownst to them, their rejoinder to the expression of a new idea is almost totally negative. This discussion is designed to consider ten typical managerial reactions to such an expression.

1. Who Dreamed It Up?

Consider for a moment how many times during the past year you have used the phrase, "Who ever dreamed up that idea?" It is highly probable that this phrase was used to express your reaction to the expression of a new idea.

While the phrase contains no negative terms, its likely interpretation is negative. For example, this reaction is most often interpreted to mean, "Who (could be so dumb as to have) ever dreamed up that (ridiculous) idea?" Is there any doubt as to why the person on the receiving end of this expression feels somewhat rebuffed? Of course not, and the person submitting the suggestion is not likely to use the suggestion box again. Sure, he may continue to generate new ideas, but he may lack the courage to express them.

I was invited to consult for a company that deals in software that needed to increase its efficiency quickly to survive. A new manager was hired to bring about the necessary change. He requested for a system to be established as a way to capture their ideas.

On our third day of framing up ideas, we came across a particular one that caught our attention. It was submitted by one of the staff and it was referring to the CEO of the organization squandering the company's profit on promiscuity. We laughed about it but we couldn't discourage or report such employee in order not to discourage him/her from submitting more ideas.

The next time you are confronted with a new idea try this phrase instead: "Thank you for your suggestion. Do you have more information as to how this idea might be useful?" This reaction contains no commitment on your part and encourages the person with the idea to devote more serious thoughts.

2. Is it Saleable?

If your firm is engaged in sales, probably the most common rejoinder to a new idea is, "It's too hard to sell." On what basis do you make such a hasty statement?

How do you know it will be difficult to sell if you have never tried it? These will be the questions generated in the mind of the person making the suggestion. Again he will become discouraged and feel that management has made a conclusion too hastily

Had your reaction been, "Thanks, we shall immediately determine its salability," the person with the idea would be encouraged by the understanding that his suggestion was being taken seriously.

3. Considerate Avoidance

How often have you used or heard the phrase, "I'll appoint a committee to study it?" Again, this is not a negative statement when interpreted literally. However, submitting an idea to a committee for study may easily be interpreted to mean the matter will be placed under investigation for the next twenty years or so. As we all know, the committee system has its advantages and disadvantages. One of the latter is its inherent ability to postpone indefinitely or totally bury an issue before proper consideration is given. Suggesting that an idea be submitted to a committee may, at times, be described as considerate avoidance.

If an idea does warrant committee consideration, place some definite constraints on how it will be handled. Explain to the idea generator why it is being channeled to a committee, how and when it will be studied. Finally, offer some assurance that the results of the committee study will be communicated back to the idea originator. Remember, if the person becomes discouraged with your reaction to his idea, he may withhold his next idea and it may be the one in 100,000 that you have been waiting for and have need of.

4. Resistance to Change

New ideas often pertain to changes in operational procedures. The suggestion may be relevant to a change in your accounting procedures, your inventory and credit policy, or even something as mundane as the way in which your customers are greeted over the telephone. If a new idea does imply a change in a long established business procedure, one's reaction to it may be of the type, "That's not the way we did it in the past." This phrase is comparable to saying, "Who needs improvement?"

This is the most frequent answer I have received from individuals or organizations. Any time, I ask why something can't be done in another way, the patented response often is: "Because that's how we've been doing things!" It is difficult to work or argue with logic like that!

Management or individuals often fail to realise that the status quo becomes second best immediately upon the development and availability of an improved procedure. This is not to say that new ideas continually should be adopted purely for the sake of change; new ideas should however not be perfunctorily tossed out solely on the basis that they would require a change in procedure.

Had your rejoinder been, "Thank you, your suggestion may result in some much-needed changes," the originator would understand that his idea is appreciated and that it will be given a fair hearing. At no time should the idea recipient imply that the status quo retains a competitive advantage over a suggested change.

5. Too Costly

In the business world, there is probably no more effective way to kill new ideas than the use of the phrase, "It's going to cost money." Of course it will cost money! Good ideas cost money in the beginning. The development of the computer, jet engine, and nuclear power were all very costly endeavors. However, the savings which ultimately evolved from these new ideas far surpassed the development costs and rendered alternate sources of computation, travel and energy (respectively) obsolete.

Ask yourself, "When did you ever earn a Naira without first investing a Naira?" The merits of a new idea must not be judged on costs alone. Your reaction to the suggestion should imply that while costs are important, savings and eventual revenues will be given equal consideration.

6. We Tried It Once
Another common management rejoinder is, "That's been tried before." If this typifies your reaction to a suggestion, you are dodging the issue. This dodge is often successful in that it suggests to the idea generator that he is incapable of developing a truly original idea. Even if the management is not attempting to dodge the issue and the idea has, in fact, been tried before, the situation may have changed. What proved unsuccessful before may turn out to be a real bonanza under the new environment.

Your reaction should have been phrased, "This idea reminds me of something we tried before, but it may be worthy of a second look and another attempt." This does not kill the idea, but places it in the proper perspective. The person submitting the suggestion feels assured that his idea is not being dodged and that management is not relying solely on hindsight to render its judgment. Consider for a moment what might have happened to the men's fashion designer who, about a year ago, suggested to his employer that the firm might manufacture flashy, wide ties for men. Had the management relied on the past trends and hindsight, the suggestion would have been ignored and the firm might have badly missed the market.

7. It's too Complex

"It's too complicated," is another management rejoinder, which may imply an attempt to avoid the issue. President J. F. Kennedy once suggested that the USA should have a man on the moon by 1970. Many people, including numerous scientists, discounted this suggestion on the basis that the feat would be much too complicated to achieve in such a short time. Those fearful of the complexity have now been shown to be erroneous. Mankind can attain miraculous achievements with determination, hardwork and devotion to duty. But without new ideas, regardless of how complex they may be, mankind is unable to set the goals towards which his efforts can be directed.

If a new idea requires complex changes, be honest in your expression of this fact. However, do not allow complexity alone to detract from the value of the idea nor deter you from conducting a complete analysis of the idea's prospects. Once this is communicated to the person submitting the new idea, he will be satisfied that his contribution is being handled properly.

8. Whose Problem?

Suggestions or new ideas need not necessarily be related to your line of business. For example, suppose you are the manager of a feed manufacturing plant and an employee approaches you with an idea for improving the durability of sprinkler irrigation systems. What would be your reaction to his idea? "It's not our problem," is a possible rejoinder. In expressing this reaction, the management is also implying that they decline any interest in the profit which might evolve from the sprinkler improvement. Having received management's reaction, the employee with the idea will either quietly withdraw or, worse yet, become disgruntled and take his idea to one of your competing feed manufacturers who is more open-minded about diversifying his operations.

I met a mechanical engineer at the airport on one of my trips and a hot debate ensued between us. I explained to him fascinating things I could do with the organization he worked for by setting up an IMS for them. He said out right, "management problem is not my problem. They give me a job and I'll do it. Finish!" I tried to convince him but he shocked me with his response "they (the management) told me so themselves."

Instead of reacting negatively, the management should recognize that while the new idea lies outside the present scope of operations, it may prove attractive enough to warrant further consideration as a diversified activity.

9. Complacency

The ninth common managerial reaction to new ideas is characterized by the phrase, "We're doing all right without it." Perhaps the firm is doing well at the present time, but can management accurately predict the future? Will good times continue? Can your firm afford to remain static in a dynamic society? If management fails to openly express an interest in improvement, the future will likely become that firm's major adversary. To guard against the uncertainties of the future, management must remain on the lookout for all potential improvements. It is human nature to become more complacent during a period of favourable economic conditions.

Complacency, however, is a very expensive luxury, which few businesses can afford. Listen carefully to the new idea with which you are confronted and compliment the source of the idea by using the phrase, "We are always looking for helpful suggestions; yours will be given serious thought."

10. The Risk

The acceptance of a new idea does involve a risk. This is an indisputable fact. But risk alone, should not be used by management as the scapegoat for the avoidance of promising suggestions. How often have you used the phrase, "It's never been tried before and is therefore, too risky?" Consider for a moment how boring life, itself, would be if risk and uncertainty were nonexistent.

This is a logical explanation only if you lack the imagination for change or the courage to respond to a risk. I am not suggesting that unwarranted risks be taken in the ambitious pursuit of new ideas, but that some risk is inherent in all activities, which have never been tried before. Risk becomes one of many factors which must be studied when the management evaluates a new idea. Once the management is aware of the risks involved, contingency plans can be formulated to guard against that rare catastrophe.

All business ventures involve some degree of risk. The acceptance of new ideas is no different. The management should express its willingness to try something new, given proper recognition of the risks involved.

And a fatal but
In fact most suggestion boxes fail after 12 to 18 months for the same reasons:

A
A well promoted suggestion box leads to an initial surge of idea submissions. However, with no indication of what kinds of ideas are wanted, the scheme is typically inundated with all kinds of ideas, many of them totally irrelevant to business needs. The managers in charge of reviewing ideas cannot process them in a timely manner, leaving idea submitters to believe that their suggestions are being ignored. As a result, employees come to believe that submitting ideas is a waste of time.

B
Particularly in opaque suggestion schemes, there is a tendency to receive many duplicate ideas. These are often inspired by television programs and articles in trade journals widely read by employees. Nevertheless, duplicate ideas take time to process and this exacerbates Suggestion Overflow.

C

Because suggestion schemes do not indicate what kinds of ideas should be submitted, many that are submitted are irrelevant to current business needs and as a result must be rejected. A high level of rejections sends the message that although management claims innovation is important, they are not really interested in ideas because they reject so many of them!

Ironically, while suggestion schemes have a tendency to capture many ideas that may be good, but which are not related to business needs, many managers are often in urgent need of innovative business ideas - but are not getting any relevant ones.

The logical approach then would be to tell employees what kinds of ideas you want. That would focus their creative thinking on current business needs.

In short, they are imagining a modern suggestion box. But instead of a box with a slot, employees are provided with a software interface for submitting ideas. This will be ultimately dealt with in Chapter 6: Business and Idea

Although there are variations on how suggestion schemes process ideas, nearly all involve an individual or team who review submitted ideas and decide whether or not to develop them further. The software normally includes tools to automate the review process.

The best suggestion schemes will be transparent, allowing idea submitters to review their own and other ideas as well as comment on ideas. However, many schemes are opaque. Ideas are submitted directly to the reviewers and no one can see what happens to them thereafter.

At first glance, the suggestion scheme seems a simple yet effective approach to capturing ideas from the workforce. After all, employees have ideas - all you need is a tool to capture and evaluate those ideas.

Key points:

1. Suggestion boxes have been around for decades. Yet most people do not believe that anyone ever actually reads ideas dropped into a suggestion box. For the most part, this is because once an idea is dropped into a suggestion box, the submitter is unlikely to ever see it again – hence she assumes no one is interested in her idea.

   Sadly, many suggestion scheme idea management solutions suffer a similar reputation.

2. The sad fate of many suggestion schemes is that they sit idle full of ideas that no one is processing. Meanwhile employees doubt that anyone is interested in their ideas (because they are not being processed) and so stop submitting them.

3. The discussion suggests means by which the managerial reactions can be rephrased so as to encourage the development, study and acceptance of new ideas. Successful managers are as willing to listen as to talk.

4. The rapid acceptance of new ideas has been, and continues to be of vital importance to the success of businesses. Management cannot ignore the theory of the suggestion box. All too often managers unknowingly discourage the generation of new ideas within their firms. This discouragement often appears in the form of negative rejoinders to the expression of suggestions.

Generating Business ideas

- This chapter will open your eyes to ways to get those ideas that are lurking around you and you never get to catch them.
- It will show you how to get ideas from problems and opportunities. How you can recycle or build on any useful existing ideas.
- It also shows why frustration is good. How you can get ideas from your pain points.

It is fatal to assume that creativity deserves success
- Tomisin Ajiboye

Will Sutton, a notorious bank robber in the 1930s, supposedly was asked once why he robbed banks. His answer was simple and to the point: "Because that's where the money is!" It is as simple as that - solving a problem.

The ultimate goal of generating ideas is to state a problem in such a way that it will produce the most innovative, optimal results.

There is no intention to persuade you on how to think; rather, the focus is on clarifying some desired innovation problem involving perceptions of current and desired states.

In this chapter, I will take you on a ride through feasible techniques to help you generate ideas using the best problem solving techniques and framing up business ideas. And, to make our journey smooth we must know where we are coming from for a safe landing.

The evolution of idea management
Idea generation, or the act of generating novel, applicable ideas, is the activity most frequently associated with creative problem solving. As the ideas generated in this stage are used throughout the creative process, taking the idea generation phase seriously is crucial to the success of the Creative Problem Solving process. Efforts have been made to increase the number of ideas generated by creative professionals because a direct relationship between the number of initial ideas produced and the quality of the final idea has been established.

There are various means of generating business ideas but this book will focus mainly on individual business idea generation system. Nevertheless, I shall quickly share my experiences in accumulating business ideas in organizational idea generating systems.

1. Organizational Business Idea Generating Systems:

Increasingly, companies will compete based on the speed at which they can discover, develop and implement ideas for new products and services. To compete at this level, organisations must efficiently tap into the creativity of all of their employees. Not only that, but they must also be adept at focusing employees' creative energies around key business issues: gathering and evaluating ideas efficiently, and quickly identifying those with the greatest bottom-line potential for implementation.

Idea management for organisations has improved to the level of software technology. These applications enable companies to solicit targeted ideas from all their employees - regardless of their geographical location - and gather them into a centralized database where it will be evaluated. This new type of enterprise can help to make such an innovation strategy possible. Idea management systems (IMS) also provide structured processes for evaluating and sharing ideas, so managers can quickly zero in on those with the greatest potential. And these are what will help many organizations to achieve every time using profound applicable tools.

As innovation grows in importance as a competitive advantage, IMS are poised to become the catalyst that can help companies to compete at levels never before possible.

Idea management for organizational systems typically offers these features and capabilities:

Campaign focused: Organisations can set up specific "campaigns" or projects within the software, each one tailored to address a specific business objective -- such as reducing costs in a division, or coming up with new ideas for a particular product line. Focused ideation around specific business objectives tends to result in a larger number of high quality ideas.

Customizable forms for capturing ideas: Organisations can customize idea input forms by campaigning or projecting to meet their specific needs.

Customizable evaluation criteria: IMS also enable companies to create customized numeric scales for evaluating ideas for each campaign. This increases the likelihood that all ideas will be rated consistently.

Collaboration and idea sharing: The leading idea management systems make it possible for employees to view the disposition of their own ideas, as well as add comments to others' ideas: using peer review processes that help to shape raw ideas into more complete, compelling solutions. Many of these Web-based idea management tools allow employees at multiple locations to share best practices quickly, around the country or around the world! Other idea management tools employ online discussion areas and other forms of collaboration to help employees build existing ideas into more powerful solutions.

Collaboration is an essential element of organisational innovation. When a team come together to devise and develop ideas, they can potentially be much more innovative than any individual member of the team can be on his/her own.

However, to be effective, a team must comprise a variety of people with different backgrounds and areas of expertise. In a corporate setting, this requires, at minimum, that a team is made up of people from different divisions within the company. At best, those people will also come from different locations or countries. As a rule of thumb: a greater variety of people participating in the idea generation process equals a higher level of creativity and innovation.

Google hasn't always been such a goldmine. In fact, when they started, Google's co-founders Larry Page and Sergey Brin weren't even sure how their site would make money.

At the time, several rudimentary search tools existed, but a search on one of them would generally yield thousands of results, which were not ranked in any order of relevance. These two combined minds to detect and discuss the problem, then combined resources to develop solutions in what led to Google today. Ever since, it has been improved upon, pitching their strength on their collaboration.

Recognizing each other's strength and sourcing for teams all over the world gave the organisation a huge boost within a short time.

Regardless of their features, all IMS share one common goal: To quickly locate the veritable needle in the haystack –the handful of killer ideas in a sea of mediocre ones and to shepherd them through evaluation and onto implementation. Speed to market is critical to building competitive advantage.

Benefits of organisational IMS
Idea management tools offer a number of compelling benefits to companies of all sizes:

They focus employees' creative efforts around specific organisational goals and objectives. Research by two leading suppliers of idea management systems – Bright Ideas Inc. and General Ideas - shows that when employees are asked to generate ideas or suggestions around a specific business problem or objective, the quantity and quality of ideas tends to increase significantly.

They encourage employees to capture all of their ideas. In most types of businesses, employees rarely capture their ideas, and most of their "eurakas!" are lost forever. IMS help to solve this problem.

Employees can now quickly jot down the germs of idea, and will be able to return to the system later to add details to the new ideas they have created. In addition, many idea management tools will help employees to share ideas, comment on ideas, add to ideas, further improve on each other's ideas, and acquire knowledge by viewing the ideas of others.

IMS help companies to share best practices. For companies that have multiple offices or locations, IMS enable them to quickly and cost-effectively share ideas and best practices that have been used successfully at one location with other locations. This allows them to multiply the bottom-line benefit of a single cost-saving idea many times over. Usually, corporate locations or divisions operate like silos, rarely sharing information, ideas and best practices.

They help companies to increase their speed to market. Idea management systems help companies to capitalize on their best ideas faster. They do so by providing a structured process for evaluating ideas and selecting the best for implementation, and by providing a set of checks and balances to make sure that all ideas are promptly reviewed and evaluated.

They can be used in many types of common corporate applications. Idea management systems do not only provide a valuable tool set for developing new product and service ideas, but can also catalyze greater results from corporate cost-reduction initiatives. You can also invite outside partners, such as suppliers, dealers and joint venture partners, to contribute ideas.

In conclusion, organisational idea management systems are an idea whose time has come. Because they are Web-based, they enable organisations to gather, share and evaluate ideas with a speed and flexibility never before possible. This, in turn, can help corporations to compete at a new, higher level, surprise and delight customers in exciting new ways. Best of all, idea management systems enable managers to measure the bottom-line impact of ideas collected and implemented, making it easier than ever before to determine the "return on ideas" that these idea management systems provide.

2. Individual Business Idea Generating System:

Alex F. Osborn (*The Father of **Brainstorming***) stated that out of the entire creative problem solving process, individuals are likely to experience the greatest difficulty during idea generation. This is partly due to the fact that it is difficult for individuals to suspend judgment when formulating ideas. Individuals tend to focus more on the quality of the idea and the practicability, as opposed to focusing on generating as many ideas as possible.

The creative process is also inhibited by people's inability to entertain ideas that violate previously held assumptions, rules and conventions. In other words, individuals must be able to break associations and patterns of thoughts in order to create new relationship that didn't previously exist. Additionally, the idea generation process is heavily influenced by intrinsic motivation. This implies that creative professionals must be given both the tools and the incentives to produce creative works.

In order to help individuals in the idea generation process, I have identified methods to stimulate creative thought, generate more ideas and expand on the solution space. These strategies categorize the methods used by creative professionals in pursuit of the creative end product. Idea generation strategies consist of a mixture of artificial formal techniques and classifications of naturally occurring design practices. These strategies will be well discussed in this part of the book.

Are you ready?

Strategy #1
Do What You Love

How much are you supposed to like what you do? Unless you know that, you don't know when to stop searching – **Paul Graham**

I remember when we used to make a certain joke in my office; any money or cheque paid was referred to as "stupid" money. This was no form of an abuse or disrespect towards any client but it was culled from the fact that we were just enjoying what we do and getting paid hugely for enjoying ourselves. We did not arrive there overnight; it took us many jobs we did excellently well, endurance, persistency and consistency.

To do something well, you have to like it. That idea is not exactly novel. I've got it down to four words: "Do what you love." But it's not enough just to tell people that. Doing what you love is complicated.

The very idea is foreign to what most of us learn as kids. When I was a kid, it seemed as if work and fun were opposite by definition. Life had two states: some of the time adults were making you do things, and that was called work; the rest of the time you could do what you wanted, and that was called playing. Occasionally, the things adults made you do were fun, just as, occasionally, playing wasn't—for example, if you fell and hurt yourself. But except for these few anomalous cases, work was pretty much defined as not-fun.

And it did not seem to be an accident. School, it was implied, was tedious *because* it was preparation for grownup work.

The world then was divided into two groups, grownups and kids. Grownups, like some kind of cursed race, had to work. Kids didn't, but they did have to go to school, which was a diluted version of work meant to prepare us for the real thing. Much as we disliked school, the grownups all agreed that grownup work was worse, and that we had it easy.

Teachers in particular seemed to believe implicitly that work was not fun. Which is not surprising: work wasn't fun for most of them. Why did we have to memorize state capitals instead of playing dodge ball? For the same reason they had to watch over a bunch of kids instead of lying on a beach. You couldn't just do what you wanted.

I'm not saying we should let little kids do whatever they want. They may have to be made to work on certain things. But if we make kids to work on dull stuff, it might be wise to tell them that tediousness is not the defining quality of work, and indeed that the reason they have to work on dull stuff now is a preparedness to working on more interesting stuff later.

When I was about 9 or 10, my father told me I could be whatever I wanted when I grew up, so long as I enjoyed it. I remember that precisely because it seemed so anomalous. It was like being told to use dry water. Whatever I thought he meant, I didn't think he meant work could *literally* be fun—fun like playing. It took me years to grasp that.

I have always been a big proponent of following your heart and doing exactly what you want to do. It sounds so simple, right? But there are people who spend years, decades, even trying to find a true sense of purpose for themselves. My advice; Just find the thing you enjoy doing more than anything else, your one true passion, do it for the rest of your life, at nights and weekends when you're exhausted and cranky and just want to go to bed.

It could be anything – music, writing, drawing, acting, teaching – it really doesn't matter. All that matters is that once you know what you want to do, you dive in a full 10 percent and spend the other 90 torturing yourself because you know too well that it's far too late to make a drastic career change, and that you're stuck on this mind-numbing path for the rest of your life.

Is there any other way to live?

Before you get started, though, you need to find one interest or activity that truly fulfills you in a way nothing else can. Then, really immerse yourself in it for a few fleeting moments after an exhausting 10 hour day at your desk job and an excruciating 65-minute commute home. During nights when all you really want to do is lie down and shut your eyes for a few precious hours before you have to drag yourself out of bed for work the next morning, or on weekends when your friends want to hang out and you're dying to just lie on your couch and watch TV because you're too fatigued to even think straight – these are the times when you need to do what you enjoy most in life.

Here is a way out.

Starting a successful new business takes time. Lots of time. So, as you begin to think about compelling new business ideas, none are more important to consider than those related to your areas of passion. If you're going to invest the long hours it takes to plan and successfully run a new business, it is absolutely critical that you are passionate and get excited about the business concept you ultimately embrace. Your passion naturally translates into every aspect of your business.

If you lack passion for the new business, your planning effort will certainly be stunted. Dispassion about your business will ooze out in nearly every area of your business – making it even harder for you to generate investment funding, hire good employees and earn revenue. In a competitive market place, dispassion can nearly condemn a new business to failure even before it starts.

Passionate entrepreneurs have an edge.

When you talk to a truly successful entrepreneur, you will notice something distinctive about how they describe their business. They speak in passionate terms about what they do and how they do it, showing both the heart and brain power necessary to become successful. If we are truly lucky in life, we find a life's calling that makes us want to get up and get going every morning and makes it hard for us to leave the office at night.

We all have equal amounts of time, but the continuous ideas invested in your business can influence it widely. Getting back to the role passion plays, there is nothing more attractive than someone who is on fire because they are passionate about their work and the experiences they create for others.

When you're passionate, you'll be much more willing to invest the time it takes to create the right strategy and execute it successfully. Why not create a business that motivates you to wake up early, stay up late, and provides a sense of fulfillment? How do you identify your areas of passion and how do you turn that into a business of doing what you love? The following tools will walk you through, step by step, in a simple and easy format that will help you generate new business ideas that hone in on your top areas of passion.

Robyn Green had been frustrated at her work for many months and did not know what else to do. But she did one thing every day after work to unwind. She went to the cinema every night to see a movie. Her thought was, 'if I end my day with frustration and stress, I can at least not resume with it every morning.'

One late afternoon when Robyn went to the movie theatre she noticed a mom with a baby a few seats away. During the movie the baby began to howl. Robyn began to think what a pity that the mother was there alone and had to endure the scorn of other movie patrons who didn't appreciate the crying. "Wouldn't it be nice if she could come to the movie with all her friends and their babies too?" She envisioned a place where moms (and dads) could watch movies with their newborn film critics and not worry about a little crying here or there. As Robyn walked around her community, she stopped every mom she saw with a baby and asked if this concept would interest them and "99 moms out of 100 totally lit up and loved the idea." So, she rented space in an independent movie theatre and started Movies for Mommies to make her baby-friendly, movie-going experience a reality – complete with stroller parking, bottle warming, and changing tables. Robyn has since turned her passion for movies into new locations all across Canada, to the delight of thousands of moms. Ever since, she can't recall a single day that she felt stressed or frustrated because of a switched from her work to fun.

Generating Ideas: Doing what you love.

1. Write your answers to the following questions to identify some of your top areas of passion:
- How do you like to spend your weekends?
- If a long-lost rich uncle wrote you a cheque for N5, 000,000 how would you then spend your time? (After any initial travel and shopping sprees are done)
- What kind of magazines do you like to read?
- What kind of websites do you like to visit?
- What would you do if you knew it was absolutely impossible to fail?

2. Each of these answers indicates some of your top areas of interest and passion. Circle your top two areas of passion from this list above.

3. Copy each of these top two areas of passion onto the top of the following pages.

4. Write down all of the steps associated with each activity in the STEPS column on the next page

(See example below as a guide).

5. Then, as you look at each step ask yourself 'what do you find annoying or frustrating about this step?' This will help you identify pain points associated with each step. Write down these pain points in the PAIN POINTS column

FOR EXAMPLE, if you identified playing football as one of your top areas of passion, some of the steps associated with playing football games and pain points associated with each step may be:

Steps	Pain Points
Join a training team	There is none near me
Buy kits	They are very expensive

Following the examples listed above, list your top areas of passion, steps for completing each activity, and associated pain points on the following pages.

AREA OF PASSION #1: _____

Steps	Pain Points

6. Circle your top four most painful pain points and label them numbers 1 to 4. Write below how each pain point will be addressed 2 years from now? How will it be addressed 5 years from now?

Solutions to
1st pain point:

Solutions to
2nd pain point:

Solutions to

3rd pain point:

Solutions to
4th pain point:

7. Each of these pain points and solutions are actually customer needs that form the foundation of new business ideas. Circle the top new business idea in your list to review later.

8. Repeat the previous steps on the next page with your other top area of passion.

AREA OF PASSION #2: _____

Steps	Pain Points

9. Circle your top four most painful pain points and label them numbers 1 to 4. Write below how each pain point will be addressed 2 years from now? How will it be addressed 5 years from now?

Solutions to
1st pain point:

Solutions to
2nd pain point:

Solutions to
3rd pain point:

Solutions to
4th pain point:

10. Each of these pain points and solutions are actually customer needs that form the foundation of new business ideas. Circle the top new business idea in your list to review later.

11. You now have several new business ideas you can come back to, evaluate, and build on. If you'd like to generate more business ideas then continue with Strategy #2 on the following page. If you have already generated all the business ideas you need you can jump to the idea evaluation on the next section

> I'd like to say that if you can get this first phase right, it will be happily ever after for you and your new business idea, but there will be many mountains to climb. So it will be difficult at times, but it is far more important that you are happy and get to do what you are passionate about every day than dread getting up in the morning because you dislike what you do.

For many, the 'out-of-the-box' thinking is difficult and strange. Human beings are creatures of habit and tend to do things as they've always been done, exactly how they've always been taught to do something. Unfortunately, this is very restrictive, non-creative thinking. Do you sometimes feel like the mime inside the glass box? Trapped inside and always trying to figure a way out? Try finding a creative solution to your escape. Perhaps a special key or maybe just a large hammer would do the trick. Scott Adams said, "Creativity is allowing yourself to make mistakes. Art is knowing which ones to keep."

Strategy #2:

Can't Find It? Create It!

Any runner will tell you that the right shoes are the key to success and it is this thinking that has been the driving force behind sporting goods manufacturer Adidas.

Germany after the First World War however, was a tough place to start a business but Adolf Adi Dassler was determined not to let this stop him. From a skill he learned from his father, Adi used whatever items he could scavenge to make his shoes, including parachutes and army helmets, while his sisters cut patterns out of canvas. Creativity and sheer hard graft kept the business going, as well as Adi's vision to develop the perfect running shoes. This vision encompassed three guiding principles: produce the best shoes for the requirements of the job, protect the athlete from injury and ensure the product lasted. Those are the three lines that represent the logo of Adidas.

A great business idea combines your skills with imagination and market demand. A business idea often comes from everyday problems that someone solves. Successful businesses find a need and fill it by providing a service or product. Entrepreneurs who look at ways to make an existing product or service better can be as successful as those who create or invent products.

I often meet business founders whose minds are overflowing with brilliant ideas for new products. They seem to develop terrific new concepts every single day of their lives. They are watchful, always inquiring, perceptive and continually seeking (and finding) the next big thing. Their never-ending challenge is to pick up a winner – (only one!) – out of scores of possibilities and run it.

On the other hand, I listened to intelligent and aspiring entrepreneurs who can't concoct a single viable idea. These great souls are bright and earnest, but for some reason imaginative ideas escape them.

Within my circle of friends, I see both types of individuals. One is the quintessential entrepreneur who has developed several companies and has recently launched a new firm.

The other struggles to envision the next great product everyone in Nigeria would want. From time to time, he asks me if there is a method to generate great ideas.

Today, I am happy to share with the world the process for generating world-class business ideas.

When I first came up with this tool some few months back, it was an IMS breakthrough because of its easy and yet effective model. A testing ground was set and it was a massive success. From then, I knew that over time it was going to be a remarkable product in market. Every other success story with my clients and students was as expected.

Remarkable new product ideas are everywhere and there is a limitless supply of concepts waiting to be commercialized, launched and marketed. They are there to be seen and pursued by those who seek them. In fact, ideas are available to everyone, worldwide, and at any moment. In some cases, an innovator in Nigeria and thinker in Nairobi will be enlightened at the same moment in time.

Ideas can be small and simple, or large and complex. A passion for a subject may be the genesis of a compelling idea; derived from time enjoying a cherished hobby. A new product may result from a tinkerer who sees an opportunity to transpose an existing concept to a totally new context (this will be more discussed in next chapter). Or someone might envision blending two disparate disciplines into an entirely new field of endeavor.

For entrepreneurs who have trouble generating ideas on their own, they can look into researching ideas. There is wealth of ideas online for anyone who can develop the idea and take the products/services to market. If an entrepreneur can take a researched idea, validate it in the market place and license it, he or she can commercialize the product as though the idea were his own.

Ideas are generally developed from known facts; not from thin air. Business builders who generate bold ideas possess a high level of knowledge acquired by study, instruction and experience. Many high achievers have benefited from lessons learned from earlier educational and prior career experiences that have become foundational underpinnings of understanding.

Ideas can also be created by listening to customer needs and their perspective on new concepts; from data gathered on products manufactured and sold; from marketing research summaries; from the results gained from pilots of programs, and by observing establishes procedures. For instance, an employee may see an opportunity to start his or her new business by automating a labor intensive and costly business procedure via a software application that an entire industry may purchase.

Look around where you are. You are surrounded by business ideas. They are absolutely everywhere. Do you see them around you? No? That's ok, most people don't at first. But that doesn't change the fact that they are all around you right now. The problem is that most good business ideas are hidden. If you seek business ideas directly, they will often remain hidden. The trick is that you need to know what to look for.

Just like I told a client who wrote almost two pages of what he called complaints for me under forty three minutes. When I went through his complaints, I saw problems instead. I had to make him see and realized that his complaints were problems that had been blocking his mind from being creative about the solutions to his challenges. We often don't know what or where to look when searching for new business ideas.

The best business ideas represent solutions to problems that make things better, easier, faster, or more efficient.

Problems can take the form of frustrations, annoyances, dissatisfaction, or even anger. Generally, things that most people try to resist or avoid. Collectively, you can refer to each of these symptoms as pain points. Pain points are the catalysts for great business ideas. Since each of us has an unlimited supply of pain points, each of us has an unlimited supply of business ideas all around us.

If a person has a big enough pain point, he or she will do anything to find a solution to relieve the pain. That person is also known as a customer and that solution can form the foundation of a new business. In short, pain point is a process that begins with a situation; perhaps problem or frustration. The observer may then ask himself what is happening and why. This lead to the gathering of information followed by a thoughtful prediction that might explain the matter.

What's an easy way to spot the limitless supply of pain points all around us to help us create new business ideas? The following exercise will point you in the right direction.

Generate Ideas: Can't Find It? Create It!

1. Spend a full day hunting for pain points. This means you should take a look at all the products and services around you as you walk around your home, work, or community. As you notice each product or service, write the name of each one in the PRODUCTS/SERVICES column below.

2. Then, as you look at each one ask yourself 'what do you find annoying or frustrating about this product or service?' This will help you identify pain points with each product or service or features and attributes you simply can't find but wish you could. Write down these pain points in the PAIN POINTS column below.

PRODUCTS/SERVICES	PAIN POINTS

3. Circle your top four most painful pain points and label them numbers 1 to 4. How will this pain point be addressed 2 years from now? How will it be addressed 5 years from now? Write your proposed solutions below.

Solutions to
1st pain point:

Solutions to
2nd pain point:

Solutions to
3rd pain point:

Solutions to
4th pain point:

4. Each of these pain points & solutions are actually customer needs and business ideas. Circle the top new business ideas in your list above to review later.

5. If you'd like to generate more business ideas then continue with Strategy #3. If you have already generated all the business ideas you need you can jump to the idea evaluation section.

Strategy #3:
Tapping into Your Vast Experience

When I left my first job where I worked as a business development manager to join the team of a reputable consulting firm, my first day on the job was a major breakthrough because I had a particular experience that other co-workers didn't have.

I worked in a reputable photography organisation where they make different picture frame sizes and offer other services too. Eventually, when I arrived on my second job, the organisation was working on a project with a certain state government and my experience of picture frames was remarkably useful in suggesting a new idea that earned me respect and my place on my new job.

Vast experience is a familiarity with a skill or field of knowledge acquired over months or years of actual practice and which, presumably has resulted in superior understanding or mastery.

Experience can serve as the best channel that can make ideas generation fun. With experience, you can get closer to the action or you can easily recover ideas that you have picked along the line. One of the best places to look for new business ideas is in an industry where you have previously worked. Work experience provides a window into an industry that is much harder to see through by those who never had that work experience.

In fact, Inc magazine conducted a survey of CEOs from America's fastest-growing private businesses and found that 57% of the CEOs "got the original idea for their business by spotting an opportunity in the industry they worked in."

What should you do when you bring a good idea to your boss and your boss says "no thanks"? When that happened to Tom Golisano he decided to start his own company. He was originally working for a company that provided payroll processing services to mid-sized companies. With that narrowed target market they were ignoring the small business market which represented 95% of all businesses. Tom approached several executives where he worked about a proposal to start targeting small businesses. They each said no. Tom said goodbye to the old employer and started Paychex to provide payroll processing services to small businesses. It turned out to be a good idea. Paychex is now the second largest payroll processor in America.

You don't have to work in a leadership role or an executive position within a business or company to gain valuable insight into what some customer or employee pain points may be. Front line workers who have regular contact with customers are also in an excellent position to spot opportunities. Even in business development, the role of idea generation cannot be neglected from product and services to the creation of marketing strategies, to the generation of sales leads, to negotiating and closing deals. The job of experience helps identify new business ideas, whether that means new markets, new partnerships with other business ideas, new ways to reach existing markets and then go out and exploit those new opportunities.

Have you worked in a few companies before? If so, then the following exercise can help you spot new opportunities within those same industries.

Generate Ideas: Tap into Your Vast Experience

1. Write the name of the most recent company where you have worked in the NAME OF COMPANY section.

NAME OF COMPANY #1

PRODUCTS/SERVICES/PROCESSES	PAIN POINTS

2. List the primary products or services sold by this company or any key processes within the company in the PRODUCTS/SERVICES/PROCESSES column above.

3. As you look at each product, service, or process, ask yourself 'what did customers or employees not like about this product, service, or process?' This will help you identify pain points associated with each product or service. Write down these pain points in the PAIN POINTS column above.

4. Circle your top three most painful pain points listed on the previous page and label them numbers 1 to 3. What could you do to resolve each pain point? How will each pain point be solved in 2 years? How will each pain point be solved in 5 years? Write your proposed solutions below.

Solutions to 1st pain point:
Solutions to 2nd pain point:
Solutions to 3rd pain point:

5. Each of these pain points and solutions are actually customer needs and business ideas. Circle the top new business ideas in your list above to review later.

6. Repeat this process for additional companies where you have worked on the following pages. This will help you better analyze products, pain points, and potential solutions within each related industry.

7. Remember the key steps to finding opportunities at places you've worked are to:
• Write the name of the company in the NAME OF COMPANY section
• List the main products or services sold by this company or key processes in the PRODUCTS/SERVICES/PROCESSES column
• Look at each product or service and ask yourself 'what did customers or employees not like about this product, service, or process?' Write down these pain points in the PAIN POINTS column

Try these steps with an additional business where you've worked on the following page.

NAME OF COMPANY #2

PRODUCTS/SERVICES/PROCESSES	PAIN POINTS

8. Circle your top three most painful pain points listed above and label them numbers 1 to 3. What could you do to resolve each pain point? How will each pain

point be solved in 2 years? How will each pain point be solved in 5 years? Write your proposed solutions below.

Solutions to
1st pain point:

Solutions to
2nd pain point:

Solutions to
3rd pain point:

9. Circle the top solutions listed above to consider later as new business ideas. If you'd like to generate more business ideas then continue with Strategy #4 on the following pages. If you have already generated all the business ideas you need you can jump to the idea evaluation.

Strategy #4:
Recycle a Business Idea from other Community ideas

This is the part where I always tell my clients the difference between porting a business idea and recycling one.

When you port any business from other communities into Nigeria, it means you would bring the business idea with its entire system as it is been run in the other communities. Customers vary as does cultural market. For instance, pork business is a popular business idea in the USA and many businesses have been built around pig. You can't just port such business idea into Nigeria business market. You will need a life time to make that happen because pork meat is only eaten by 14% of Nigerians.

If you have a vast business idea on pork business you could recycle it in the Nigerian market by substituting pork for beef since more that 80% of Nigerian eats beef.

Would you love to explore the world? Then this strategy is for you. There are amazing numbers of businesses located across the country and across the world that you don't need to plan or target customers in your community.

If these far-away businesses address customer needs that are not being sufficiently met in your community, why not consider recycling some of these good business ideas by bringing them to your community? You can improve upon these business ideas, learn from a company's strengths and weaknesses, and bring them to life in your community. You can market similar products or services to the same type of target customer or you could try targeting a completely different type of market segment.

I remember the story of Robert Johnson the original founder of Black Entertainment Television. When

Robert Johnson struck up a conversation with an aspiring entrepreneur during a taxi ride, he found that his fellow passenger had an interesting idea for a television channel for the elderly. Reading from the passenger's business plan, he found data for the population, purchasing power and consumption patterns for the elderly, reinforcing that the elderly would provide an interesting customer segment to target. Robert replied, "You could say the same thing about the black population." The passenger concurred and shared a copy of the business plan so that Robert could plug the appropriate numbers into the business plan and change "elderly" to "black." Robert, who already worked for the National Cable Television Association, approached some wealthy friends in the industry for funding. He found a receptive ear from one smart investor who saw the potential and Robert launched the Black Entertainment Television channel. In 2001 Robert sold BET to Viacom for nearly $3 billion.

Where do you find out about these interesting business ideas?

Many aspiring entrepreneurs find out about these interesting ideas while traveling or talking to friends, but the internet is a less expensive and more efficient way to learn about these business ideas from companies far away. The following exercises will help you more easily, find out about these business ideas.

Generate Ideas: Recycle a Business Idea from other Communities

1. Spend a day searching the internet to find stories of entrepreneurs who started interesting businesses that are located in another country or another state. The best places to look are smaller business newspapers.

2. As you read an article about each small business ask yourself some questions:
- What is the primary need this company appears to be trying to fill?
- Would the people in my community likely have a similar need for this type of business and could I introduce something similar locally?

If the answers are "yes" then document the business concepts below:

Name of company #1:	City & country of headquarters:	Website:
Business concept and need being filled:		
How I can improve upon this idea:		

3. Another approach is to call a member of the family or friend located far away and ask them if they know of any innovative or note-worthy businesses near where they live. Or if you are going to school far from home you can always just walk around town and see if there are any local businesses worth emulating back at home. Either way, write down a few notes about each idea

so you can add these new business concepts to the interesting ones you learned about via the internet.

4. Repeat Step 2 as you read articles or hear about other small businesses:
   • What is the primary need this additional company appears to be trying to fill?
   • Would the people in my community likely have a similar need for this type of business and could I introduce something similar locally? If the answer is "yes" then document the business concept below:

Name of company #2:	City & country of headquarters:	Website:

Business concept and need being filled:

_____

_____

How I can improve upon this idea:

_____

5. **Repeat this process in the spaces that follow:**

Name of company #3:	City & country of headquarters:	Website:

Business concept and need being filled:

_____

_____

How I can improve upon this idea:

_____

| Name of company #4: | City & country of headquarters: | Website: |

Business concept and need being filled:

How I can improve upon this idea:

Name of company #5:	City & country of headquarters:	Website:

Business concept and need being filled:

_____

_____

How I can improve upon this idea:

_____

6. Review the business concepts listed above and circle the top concept(s) that you feel are most interesting and promising.
   If you'd like to generate more business ideas then you may want to try:
   • Combining two of your existing ideas together to create an interesting new idea
   • Analyzing an industry that is rapidly growing or that you find interesting to seek what problems people in this industry may be facing and what opportunities may exist to solve these problems
   • Re-doing any of the four Strategies already reviewed in this packet to generate even more ideas
   If you have already generated all the business ideas you need you should continue on to the next chapter where you can better evaluate each of your new business ideas.

Key points:

1. As the ideas generated in this stage are used throughout the creative process, taking the idea generation phase seriously is crucial to the success of the Creative Problem Solving process.

2. Idea management for organisations has improved to the level of software technology. This new type of enterprise can help to make such an innovation strategy possible.

3. Idea generation strategies consist of a mixture of artificial formal techniques and classifications of naturally occurring design practices.

4. Before you get started though, you need to find the one interest or activity that truly fulfills you in ways nothing else can.

5. These great souls are bright and earnest, but for some reasons, imaginative ideas escape.

6. You don't have to work in a leadership role within a business to gain valuable insight into what some customer or employee pain points may be.

7. You can improve upon these business ideas, learn from a company's strengths and weaknesses and bring them to life in your community.

3

Evaluating Your Business Ideas

- How to take the feasibility study of your new idea
- Easy and quick way to evaluate your business idea.

Well begun is half done ~ Aristotle

Educator/philosopher John Dewy ("A problem well defined is half solved") has echoed Nobel Prize winner Herbert Simon's notion that a well-defined idea is a solved problem. The closer an idea frame approaches a desired goal, the more likely it is to become a solution or, at least, it has the potential to be turned into one.

Instances of this situation often occur when you have come up with potential ideas which incorporate solutions within their definitions. That is because you should defer judgment when generating ideas. Otherwise, you risk losing the potential stimulation value of even poorly worded ideas. However, once you've generated all possible ideas, you should review them and make modifications as appropriate based on the criteria discussed in this chapter as well as any others you think might apply. This chapter will discuss evaluating generated business ideas for the most situational analysis and effective creative development towards implementation.

After you generate a good number of new business ideas, you'll need to determine which ideas hold the most promise and which ideas to cross off your list.

Worthwhile business ideas must fill a customer need - but not just a little need. The best ideas fill a big nagging, aching customer need, one where the gap of dissatisfaction is so huge that the customer will do almost anything to obtain the solution you're offering. That's one of the fastest ways to motivate a person to trade some money for your goods or services.

When Steve Jobs returned to Apple Computer as it was spiraling downward, he started an evaluation process for all ideas that came through his desk and then came up with a tagline, "Think Different!" They tested assumptions about what a computer was supposed to look like. Much later, he illustrated the power of evaluation by completely upending the traditional model of how music is sold. With iTunes consumers now can download music, videos or television shows and movies.

For every great business idea, there are scores of others that just won't work. You will save yourself a great deal of time, trouble and money if you put your ideas to the test before you try to implement them. Half an hour of careful thought, an afternoon of research, or a phone conversation with a knowledgeable friend might steer you away from a flawed idea, months of wasted effort and thousands of Naira lost.

Moreover, the process of testing your ideas will help you determine the kinds of things to take into account when you're creating a business concept. Eventually, your efforts will lead you to an idea that has a solid chance of success.

Unlike giant corporations that invest huge sums of money to test potential toothpaste flavors or product names, you probably won't have to spend a lot of time or money to evaluate your ideas. If you don't know your target market (see chapter 7), however, and haven't done some basic market research, chances are you won't succeed.

Let us begin with these simple steps:

1. **Ask your friends and associates to help you evaluate the concept.** If you know successful entrepreneurs, ask them what they think of your idea. Chances are they'll think of problems you are likely to encounter. You may be willing to face those obstacles or you might decide that some of them are insurmountable.

2. **Ask potential customers how much they'd pay for your product or service.** Their answer will help you focus on your potential market and will give you a sense of how strong that market is. Once you have some answers to this question,

you can begin to estimate your prospective firm's potential revenues.

3. **Consider whether you are excited about the idea.** Will you actually enjoy the work that will be required to make your venture a success? If not, move on.

The Feasibility Study: Getting Down to Details.
If your initial research and thinking turns up positive results, begin work on a feasibility study. The study can take the form of formal documents that will help you recruit potential partners, investors, or lenders. Alternatively, however, it can be a simple memo to yourself – a series of questions designed to help you decide whether you should proceed to the next level of commitment.

Either way, your feasibility study should address the following issues, each of which will require in-depth consideration:

1. **The Product or Service:** What are its unique features? How will it be designed, manufactured, and delivered to customers?

2. **The Management Team:** Does your team have experience in the industry? What skills or qualifications are missing from the current team?

3. **The Market:** Who are the target customers? How big is the potential market? Is the market growing? What are the costs required to reach the target market?

4. **The Competition:** Who are your major competitors? Is your product or service superior to the competition? Would it be easy for competitors to duplicate your product or service? What are your competitors' strengths and weaknesses? How will competitors respond when your firm enters their market?

5. **The Cost:** What will it cost to start and run your business? Where will you raise the money from?

The AQQO Checklist

When evaluating your ideas there are four major evaluation categories you should be aware of. They are:

Acceptance of Idea Market
Customers' interests, willingness to patronize again, share of customers who are willing to participate in the new idea development.

Quality of Idea Creation
Ability of the idea market to stimulate idea creation, share of idea suggestions that were traded in the market, quality of the idea.

Quality of Idea Evaluation
Ability of idea market to improve forecasts of new product success, the ability of your idea stock to be in top 10 in its industry in time to come, consensus with experts.

Overall Performance of Idea Market
Perceived usefulness, interest for new product development, overall evaluation of the idea market, customer's recommendation of your idea markets, repetition of the idea market, willingness to participate once more, ability of idea markets to involve others in the new product development process

The factors above are not in order of importance, the checklist merely provides an easy way to remember acronym.

A business idea isn't worth the paper it is written on if you don't have a customer.

So who are the target customers for each of your business ideas? This is a critically important question to answer. The more you know about the ages, preferences, interests, and motives of your target customers, the more effectively you can tailor your goods or services to meet their needs. Only then are you in a position to find a way to reach and educate them about the solutions you provide to the problems they face.

The following activities will walk you through an easy way to quickly evaluate new business ideas.

1. For each of the best business ideas you generated and circled in the previous chapter of this book, write each idea in the BUSINESS IDEA sections of the following pages (one idea per section). This will make it easier to evaluate each idea quickly.

2. In the section below, write your answers to the three key questions listed about your first business idea clearly and concisely:
a. What is the compelling need that is not currently being met?
b. What is the target market that has this need (demographics, characteristics, etc.)?
c. Does this idea sound interesting and exciting to you? If so, why?

BUSINESS IDEA #1 - Clearly describe the idea in a few sentences:	Rate each answer from 1-10:
a. What is the compelling need that is not currently being met?	
b. What is the target market that has this need (demographics, characteristics, etc.)?	
c. Does this idea sound interesting and exciting to you? If so, why?	
Total Score (a+b+c):	

3. Then rate each of your answers from 1-10 in the "Rate each answer from 1-10" column on the right. An outstanding idea with a compelling need should be rated a

10; an idea with a clearly defined target market should be rated a 10; an incredibly interesting and exciting idea should be rated a 10. Anything less should be rated lower. A rating of 1 is the lowest rating. Most answers will likely fall in-between and should be rated accordingly. So, rate each answer listed above.

4. Add your three ratings together to comprise your total score (maximum total score is 30) which you should write in the shaded TOTAL SCORE section above for future comparison.

5. Repeat this process of answering the three key questions, rating each answer, and obtaining a total score for each of your business ideas listed on the pages.

BUSINESS IDEA #2 - Clearly describe the idea in a few sentences:	Rate each answer from 1-10:
a. What is the compelling need that is not currently being met?	
b. What is the target market that has this need (demographics, characteristics, etc.)?	
c. Does this idea sound interesting and exciting to you? If so, why?	
Total Score (a+b+c):	

BUSINESS IDEA #3 - Clearly describe the idea in a few sentences:	Rate each answer from 1-10:
a. What is the compelling need that is not currently being met?	
b. What is the target market who has this need (demographics, characteristics, etc.)?	
c. Does this idea sound interesting and exciting to you? If so, why?	
Total Score (a+b+c):	

BUSINESS IDEA #4 - Clearly describe the idea in a few sentences:	Rate each answer from 1-10:
a. What is the compelling need that is not currently being met?	
b. What is the target market who has this need (demographics, characteristics, etc.)?	
c. Does this idea sound interesting and exciting to you? If so, why?	
Total Score (a+b+c):	

BUSINESS IDEA #5 - Clearly describe the idea in a few sentences:	Rate each answer from 1-10:
a. What is the compelling need that is not currently being met?:	
b. What is the target market who has this need (demographics, characteristics, etc.)?	
c. Does this idea sound interesting and exciting to you? If so, why?	
Total Score (a+b+c):	

BUSINESS IDEA #6 - Clearly describe the idea in a few sentences:	Rate each answer from 1-10:
a. What is the compelling need that is not currently being met?	
b. What is the target market who has this need (demographics, characteristics, etc.)?	
c. Does this idea sound interesting and exciting to you? If so, why?	

	Total Score (a+b+c):	
BUSINESS IDEA #7 - Clearly describe the idea in a few sentences:	Rate each answer from 1-10:
a. What is the compelling need that is not currently being met?	
b. What is the target market who has this need (demographics, characteristics, etc.)?	
c. Does this idea sound interesting and exciting to you? If so, why?	
	Total Score (a+b+c):	

BUSINESS IDEA #8 - Clearly describe the idea in a few sentences:	Rate each answer from 1-10:
a. What is the compelling need that is not currently being met?	
b. What is the target market who has this need (demographics, characteristics, etc.)?	
c. Does this idea sound interesting and exciting to you? If so, why?	
	Total Score (a+b+c):	

BUSINESS IDEA #9 - Clearly describe the idea in a few sentences:	Rate each answer from 1-10:
a. What is the compelling need that is not currently being met?	

b. What is the target market who has this need (demographics, characteristics, etc.)?	
c. Does this idea sound interesting and exciting to you? If so, why?	
Total Score (a+b+c):	

BUSINESS IDEA #10 - Clearly describe the idea in a few sentences:	Rate each answer from 1-10:
a. What is the compelling need that is not currently being met?	
b. What is the target market who has this need (demographics, characteristics, etc.)?	
c. Does this idea sound interesting and exciting to you? If so, why?	
Total Score (a+b+c):	

6. Review the TOTAL SCORE for each of your business ideas. Did you rate a TOTAL SCORE of 26 - 30 for any of your ideas? If so, circle these top rated idea(s). Congratulations! These ideas may very well be worth launching into a real business and certainly warrant careful consideration.

7. Did you rate a TOTAL SCORE of 15 - 25 for any of your ideas? Don't give up on these ideas yet. These ideas may have some interesting components but there is something about each of these ideas that probably needs to be addressed. Review each of these ideas once again. Is there some way you could strengthen, add clarity to, or otherwise adjust any of these ideas to make them worthy of a 26 - 30 TOTAL SCORE? Is there some way you could build on any of these ideas to make them better match your own personal goals? Adjust your idea(s) accordingly.

Market research, Revenues, Target market

Market research: While there are many ways to perform market research, most businesses use one or more of the five basic methods: surveys, focus groups, personal interviews, observation, and field trial.

Revenues: If your sales are struggling and revenues are falling, it's essential to conduct a full review of your business to understand where things have gone wrong and where the opportunity lies for turning things around.

Target market: To make your business truly successful, you need to know who will buy your products and where your customers will come from. This preliminary research is one of the most important aspects of beginning your business.

Key points:

1. Generating new business ideas is a highly iterative process. By looking at each idea again from a fresh perspective you can always improve it. Always! The idea you thought of today can be targeted to a better niche, packaged with a better feature, or bundled with a better service to better solve customer's problems. Discuss your ideas with a trusted friend. It can be a powerful way to take a good idea today and turn it into a compelling business idea tomorrow. So, keep looking at, thinking about, and talking through your ideas. You may be able to start your new business sooner than you think.

2. Moreover, the process of testing your ideas will help you determine the kind of things to take into account when you're creating a business concept. Eventually, your efforts will help to lead you to an idea that has a solid chance of success.

3. A business idea isn't worth the paper, it is written on if you don't have a customer.

4
Implementing your Idea

- Your idea is worth nothing on paper. The world will not celebrate you for a wonderful or great idea, the world only celebrates a wonderful or great executed idea.

- The first step to it is to clarify your vision. Idea implementation must fit into the vision you have.

Let me guess – you now have more ideas for launching a new product than you can possibly implement.

After all, ideas are dime a dozen. In business, it's execution that counts.

In this chapter, I will offer some useful advice for moving your best business ideas from notion to reality.

The world is not short of ideas," says Sheahan. "It is short of people who can execute them. It is short of people who know how to take their aspirations and make a real impact on the world with them." Mostly, entrepreneurs do not have shortage of ideas, but the creative strength can quickly become a weakness if the ideas aren't managed well.

From my experience consulting for individuals and organizations, the constant messages I have always dealt with include, 'I should get moving on that.' 'What if I miss out on something big?' 'Too many ideas, too little time.' 'I wish I had the money to make this happen, it's such a great idea.' This brain-clutter will bring a truckload of great ideas to a searching halt before they even get on the road. We have come too far together on this journey to end it abruptly. Let's just do it!

Taking a systematic approach isn't always easy for the right brained, creative entrepreneur. But to get these ideas off the ground, that's what we have to do. So whether your idea is about a new product, marketing or other growth or organizational opportunities according to your evaluation, here are five "competences" that separate the dreamers from the change-makers:

1. **Packaging:** Taking your idea and transforming it into something you can sell: specific products (or services) you can offer to the marketplace.

2. **Positioning:** Aligning your offer to a market need. Even if you have to move the market (i.e., create demand from scratch).

3. **Influence:** Convincing buyers that they need this product from you – and then persuading them to part with precious time, money and energy in order to obtain it.

4. **Acceleration:** Now that you've done the really hard work, you need to get the most out of the opportunity you have created, and increase the demand for what you have to offer.

5. **Reinvention:** Leveraging your brand and expertise to open up new and bigger opportunities. (Think of computer-maker Apple leveraging its iPod base to become the dominant retailer of recorded music.)

Many entrepreneurial endeavors involve doing something that has never been done before. They need skills and clarifications that are useful in implementation and sustenance of every business idea.

Leadership
Implementing the "best" ideas for your organisation isn't about just hearing successful ideas today, but it's about your personal leadership skills – moving your organisation in the right direction for your company, with the right ideas, in the right environment and at the right time. A leader today, isn't a dictator, forcing a detailed marketing plan down employee throats. Nor, is the leader a missionary of business, fostering harmony among the various departments at all costs. Instead, a leader is more of a coach of the firm, frequently the one with the initial expertise of accomplishing the vision; the one who identifies the unmet needs of customers and clients; the one who decides the best way of fulfilling the founding vision; the one who continually rewrites that vision based on market considerations. This leader understands the reason

for the business' existence; the purpose it is destined to serve.

You must . . .
- Decide what needs to be done and how it is to be accomplished
- Continually react to market conditions, so that the vision is congruent with an ever-changing economy; and, most importantly,
- Make sure your efforts and those of your employees support that continually changing vision.

You must understand the "why" of your existence at this stage. Don't look to the sky for answers. You have to check within, check what you can do with your hands and then check with-out. Let us examine few steps to help you discover the "why".

A. Clarify Your Vision
The first step in this process is to identify and clarify your vision.

Step 1: Think of a place where you are a customer – a restaurant, where you get your hair cut; where you bank, where you truly love to do business.

Step 2: In few words, write down why you find this company so compelling; so incredibly attractive; why you continue to do business with the company.

Step 3: Now, consider what is it that you are doing; that you should be doing; or that you should be doing more of.

Past success is the enemy of our future successes. As Michael Dell, of Dell Computer, once said, "We relaxed once; I don't ever want to do that again; prosperity is very, very dangerous." Past successes will only continue to work if the market doesn't change. The problem is that not only does the market changes; it has changed and continues to change. If you're successful, you know what used to work. You can compete and succeed in markets that used to work, but what will you do tomorrow?

A profound writer, professor and management consultant, Peter Drucker said, "Show me a consistently successful company and I'll show you a company that is making courageous decisions." What does that mean? It means that we constantly need to change the things that make us successful; create an environment that supports risk and making mistakes; and encourages and accepts mistakes. We must let go of what got us to this point. This certainly takes courage; but what got you here, may keep you from getting to the next step.

B. Follow Your Vision

If you have clarity following the previous chapters, now you must follow your vision and start with an extraordinary path. What might it be? It's okay to dream! It's okay to stretch, to share those dreams with others. What might it be? To be the top of mind drycleaner in your market; in the country; in the world? Are any of these visions wrong? No. Are they extraordinary? Yes. Do they need to be? Absolutely!

In 1964 the National Aeronautics and Space Administration (NASA) in the United States had embarked on its Apollo program to land astronauts on the moon before the end of the decade. They only knew 15% of what they needed to know when they made that commitment, but the vision was extraordinary; the vision was not landing astronauts on the moon, it was "to add to human knowledge" and they have continued to succeed with that vision!

There are no shortages of good ideas, even great ones. Do they work for you? Do they fit into your vision?

- Every decision must pass through the vision statement.
- Inconsistency of performance is the biggest business killer.
- What you think about your business is, however, irrelevant; the customer's perception of what it is like to do business with you is more important.

This must start with a really good product, and from there, it moves to achieve the right fit between the company's potential and its skills, needs, and desires to create a compelling experience. It's all about the customer; and it must run through the entire organization.

C. Challenges to Decision Making Today

Paul C. Nutt wrote Why decisions Fail, and he pointed out that "decisions fail half of the time." In his research, conducted over a 2 year period, he found that 50% of all decisions made were wrong.

A classic example is the Walt Disney Company. Following the successful opening of Tokyo Disney, which broke all sorts of attendance expectations, the Disney Company turned their attention to Europe, and specifically to France for Euro Disney.

In hindsight, we know that all of the Walt Disney decisions were wrong. How could such a successful company make so many wrong decisions?

Today we have:
- Information overload
- An increasing rate of change
- Rising uncertainty
- Few historical precedents, such as the results of internet marketing
- Forced to make more frequent decisions as previously we were able to base our actions on historically based standard operating procedures; now we find they need to be customized
- Decisions seem to be more important as everything is moving so fast and when we make a decision and fail, we have to recoup our credibility
- There are conflicting goals, some are short term, others are long term, and finally,
- There are more opportunities for miscommunication; with the internet, e-mail, cell phones, voice mail and the interaction of multiple cultures.

D. Making the Decision

When Disney considered opening Euro Disney, they considered all the previous problems they had experienced.

1. In California, they had failed to buy land around the park and the area around them became fully developed so they were unable to expand.
2. In Florida, they failed to anticipate the number of hotel rooms that would be needed and lost significant potential revenues.
3. In Tokyo, they failed to get an equity position or royalties from the characters.

Keeping these issues in mind, they planned on 1 million visitors annually with ticket prices 30% higher than Orlando; they contracted for thousands of hotel rooms and estimated a 76% occupancy rate; they assumed that all visitors would have lavish sit down meals, averaging $28 per day on food and merchandise; and consistent with their family values, no alcohol was allowed in the park.

E. The Traditional Decision Making Process
Disney followed the traditional decision making process. This is generally a negative approach and tends to set a poor attitude to begin with. It will not create extraordinary decisions.

1. They defined and clarified the problem.
2. A goal or objective is defined, frequently looking for the cause of the problem
3. Options or alternatives are generated to solve the problem
4. Alternatives and tradeoffs are evaluated
5. Risks and consequences are estimated
6. A decision is made
7. Implementation begins.

This is a "how" based decision making process. This process gives you a 50% success rate, as opposed to a "why" based process.

F. Traps
There are clearly traps in this process. Traps that Disney fell into include:

1. **Perspective Traps.** We all have them, but a single one is limiting in a decision making process. Disney's perspective was to only solve problems that they had experienced elsewhere.
2. **Data traps.** Gathering data to only address the problems being considered, limits the data available from other perspectives. Data collected must provide positive and negative information from a variety of perspectives.
3. **Interpersonal traps.** In Disney's case, they forgot to ask the customer; every customer is different from the Japanese customer, the American customer as well as the European customer. For instance, occupancy was not 76%, but 36% since Paris is only 70 minutes away by train and many other areas can easily make it a day's trip. The forecasted lavish meals did not consider that Europeans like to have picnics and the lack of alcoholic beverages did not recognize the cultural attitude that alcohol is an inherent part of a meal in Europe. The door must be kept open to continually get input. Leaders can not turn people off through dictatorship.
4. **Implementation traps** are frequently the most common. Either decisions are made by not making a decision or, in haste, and with lack of knowledge; decisions are made quickly and implementation is haphazard.
5. **Unknown traps.** We cannot anticipate them all, but can recognize they will occur.

Disney wanted to sell stock on the French stock market; they lost one million dollars per day, and by 1994, they had lost over $400 million. They failed to look at the exchange rate and customers discovered that they could fly and visit Orlando for less money than Euro Disney, and the weather was a lot nicer. Disney ignored all of the warning signs using a limited perspective and little customer-specific data. This is 'how' based decision making.

G. 'Why' Based Decision Making

Disney failed to bring the magic back to decision making. As Peter Drucker says, "*The best way to predict the future is to create it*". An alternative method of making decisions is 'Why' Based. We will get what we define and what we measure.

What type of results have companies experienced with this process?
- Higher success rates of their decision making process
- Achieving faster growth rates
- Better decisions at lower levels
- Improving employee retention rates
- Higher profitability.

H. The Process
There are 4 basic steps.
1. Marshall Your Resources. All of them; gather as many perspectives as possible: engineering, production, accounting, sales, customers, suppliers, and even the government
2. The Ready Stage has two components. Consider what was successful and what should be brought forward. Ask everyone to look back on when they experienced successes. But then envisage the perfect future. This combination can provide new and unique approaches.
3. Take aim at your target. Once you have the 'why' and understanding of the vision, begin to figure out the details that it will take to implement the plan. Select the target; the direction, the wind angle, the elevation, how much powder and all factors that it will take to hit the bull's-eye.
4. Finally, fire. Execute the plan which will include the following items:
- Who is going to do it with you?
- When is it going to get done?
- Create your dashboard which will allow you to track your results.

You'll always have surprises, but you know why you're here and what you want to achieve. It's much easier to regroup.

I. The Result
A good decision making process gives you the best chance of a good outcome, but it can't be about what happened in the past. It's not about yesterday's successes. It's all about tomorrow. What are you going to do tomorrow?

Your responsibility, as leaders of your organisations, is to continuously move your company forward. I ask you to create an extraordinary vision; to take these ideas that you've read today; to create new ideas; to create a continuous, never ending cycle.

Just as the artist starts with a vision and a blank canvas or lump of clay, you have a picture in your mind of who you are and who you want to be. A painter mixes the colours in just the right way. Decide on the appropriate mix of strategies and behaviours to achieve your desired vision.

Here are simple concepts for building your market, though it will be properly discussed in Chapter 8.

- **Offer it.** (Do you admit you do not need a flat-screen TV till you saw one?)

- **Force it.** (Apple used its huge customer based to get its way in the music business.)

- **Seed it.** (Find ways to leapfrog your need product into the public eye, such as targeting celebrities.)

- **Name it.** (Put a new label on the problem you are solving.)

- **Spread it.** (Develop highly emotive stories that relate to the market need you have discovered.)

These prescriptions are more subjective than analytical, but that's to be expected. Every product, every market is different. Implementing new ideas takes more perspiration than inspiration, so, this book uses commonplace case studies to point you in the right directions, just what you need as an entrepreneur.

I took out time to emphasize on this example for the sake of better understanding. I referred to it as good because, Walt Disney Company is a successful organisation, yet, they failed in implementation of ideas. This is to open your eyes to the mistakes you don't have to make any more, taking cue from the case study. I am not saying you won't make mistakes, but it will be absolutely your own experience. You are one of a kind; therefore, no one can really predict to what heights you might soar. Even you will not know until you spread your wings!

Key points:

1. Let me guess – you now have more ideas for launching a new product than you can possibly implement.

2. Many entrepreneurial endeavors involve doing something that has never been done before. Think Salesforce.com, which promised to reform the sales-management process by proclaiming "the end of software," or the guy who invented The Pet Rock.

3. The leader understands the reason for the business' existence; the purpose it is destined to serve.

4. The first step in this process is to identify and clarify your vision.

5. If you have clarity following the previous chapters, now, you must follow your vision and start with an extraordinary path.

6. This must start with a really good product, and from there, it moves to achieving the right fit between the company's potential and its skills, needs, and desires of creating a compelling experience.

7. A good decision making process gives you the best chance of a good outcome, but it can't be about what happened in the past.

8. These prescriptions are more subjective than analytical.

You and your Idea

- In this chapter we look at a technique for objectively assessing your own strengths and weaknesses as part of the process of finding your feasible business formula.

- We look at the core competencies on which you can build your creative enterprise.

- In addition there are some thoughts about learning, training and continuing professional development.

So, you've got an idea. You've got the drive. You've got your financial ducks in a row, and they are quacking in four-part harmony. But are 'YOU' ready to start a business?

In The Art of War, Chinese military strategist Sun Tzu wrote: "If you know the enemy and know yourself, your victory will not stand in doubt."

Whether or not you regard business as a kind of warfare, his point is that knowing one's own strengths and weaknesses will help you to decide when, how and where to proceed.

It will help you recognize the customers, competition and conditions that are most likely to suit you or not. Yet 'knowing ourselves' in the sense of making objective and critical assessments of our shortcomings and special qualities is very difficult. It is much easier to assess another enterprise than our own and that's why it is useful to get outsiders' views if we are to get a clear picture of ourselves.

Knowing yourself applies not only to your personal creativity, skills and aptitudes. We need to understand the strengths and weaknesses of our business, taking into account all the people involved in the core team and wider 'family' of stakeholders including associates and advisers.

We also need to assess our assets, reputation, knowledge of the market and intellectual capital.

Evaluating Strengths and Weaknesses
Rather than simply attempting to write down all the strengths and weaknesses we can think of on a blank sheet of paper, I already devised a checklist I called The PSWA Checklist. It provides a useful structure for a comprehensive analysis and specifically for the creative business and I have used it successfully with a range of clients.

Be frank about your weaknesses too. Remember that not all weaknesses need to be fixed. Maybe, you can find a new market position where your weaknesses are not so significant. The important thing here is to recognize your strengths and weaknesses in relation to competitors. You may have a particular strength but if your competitors have it too, or are even better, then it does not give you competitive advantage.

There is more to running a successful business than ideas and resources. A number of skills and personal attributes add up to make (or break) a business owner. Knowing your strengths and weaknesses can tell you;

1. Whether you are ready to start a small business.
2. What kind of business is right for you
3. Whether you need to shore up your own skills or add a partner who can bring skills to the table that you lack.

Some of the major skill areas you will have to consider are:

Sales Skills: How are you at pricing, buying, sales planning? Are you a skillful negotiator? Do you know how to track competitors and learn from the data?

Marketing Skills: How familiar are you with advertising and public relations? Can you map out a marketing strategy and see it through?

Financial Skills: How are you at managing cash flow? (Your own chequebook might provide clues.) Can you track monthly financial data and multiple accounts? Manage credit lines, general bookkeeping, billing, payables, receivables and payroll?

Personnel Management: How will you do it when it comes to time for hiring employees? Firing them? Managing them? Motivating them?

Personal Business skills: How are you with oral and written communication, computer skills and general organisation?

The Intangibles: Do you have the ability to work hard and for long hours, to manage risk and stress, to deal with failures? Can you work well when alone and with others?

None of these are non-starters. When it comes to crucial business skills, everyone has a mix of strength and weaknesses. The trick is to recognize the areas you need to shore up before the floodwaters come.

Take a look at your own skill set with this assessment tool:

This Personal Strength and Weakness Assessment Checklist will help you identify your strength and weakness by asking you to rate yourself in several areas that are important to startups and business owners alike. Knowing your strengths and weaknesses is important because it can tell you whether you are ready to start a business, in choosing a new business, and it can tell you whether you need to consider adding a partner who can bring skills to the business that you lack.

Personal Strengths and Weaknesses Assessment Checklist

The chart below will help you identify your strengths and weaknesses and will give you a better idea of whether you're ready to become a business owner.

Examine each of the skills areas listed in the chart. Ask yourself whether you possess some or all of the skills listed in the parentheses below. Then rate your skill in each area by circling the appropriate number, using a scale of 1-5, with 1 as low, 2 as between low and medium, 3 as medium, 4 as between medium and high, and 5 as high.

Skills	Rating

	low		medium		high
	1	2	3	4	5
Sales - pricing - buying - sales planning - negotiating - direct selling to buyers - customer service follow-up - managing other sales reps - tracking competitors	1	2	3	4	5
Marketing - advertising/promotion/public relations - annual marketing plans - media planning and buying - advertising copy writing - marketing strategies - distribution channel planning - pricing - packaging	1	2	3	4	5
Financial planning - cash flow planning - monthly financial - bank relationships - management of credit lines	1	2	3	4	5
Accounting - bookkeeping - billing, payables, receivables - monthly profit and loss statements/balance sheets - quarterly/annual tax preparation	1	2	3	4	5
Administrative - scheduling - payroll handling - benefits administration	1	2	3	4	5
Personnel management - hiring employees - firing employees - motivating employees	1	2	3	4	5

▪ general management skills					
Personal business skills ▪ oral presentation skills ▪ written communication skills ▪ computer skills ▪ word processing skills ▪ fax, e-mail experience ▪ organizational skills	1	2	3	4	5
Intangibles ▪ ability to work long and hard ▪ ability to manage risk and stress ▪ family support ▪ ability to deal with failure ▪ ability to work alone ▪ ability to work with and manage others	1	2	3	4	5
Total					

After you've rated yourself in each area, total up the numbers. Then apply the following rating scale:

- If your total is less than 20 points, you should reconsider whether owning a business is the right step for you. At this level you need to consult, a professional for help and guidance before you begin anything at all.
- If your total is between 20 and 25, you're on the verge of being ready, but you may be wise to spend some time strengthening some of your weaker areas
- If your total is above 25, you're ready to start a new business now.

Competitive Advantage:
Core Competencies
This is essentially what a business does well that distinguishes it from other businesses. However, core competency can be applied to businesses of all sizes.

The origin of core competency originated as a resource-based approach to corporate strategy; it is described as something a firm can do well that meets three conditions:

1. It provides consumer benefits
2. It is not easy for competitors to imitate
3. It can be leveraged widely into many products and markets.

So, in summary, I will define core competency as key ability or strength that an organisation could acquire that will differentiate it from others, gives competitive advantage, and contributes to a long term success.

Your Core Competencies are the key skills on which you base your business success. These are often 'deeper' than first thought.

For example, Canon recognized that their core competencies were not in cameras, but more fundamentally in optics and this allowed them to see that they could transfer their expertise into the photocopier market. Similarly, Sony's core competency is not electronics but miniaturization. Honda's is not cars but engines – which helped them see beyond cars into motor boat and lawnmower markets. Richard Branson's Virgin brand is fundamentally about customer service, so, it can be applied not only to music but also to airlines, trains, financial services and mobile phones; Apple's core competence is beauty and Dangote Group's core competence is in quantity.

Some theatre companies view their core competence as 'communicating a message' using drama – rather than drama in its own right. In some cases, web designers have a core competency in branding and marketing consultancy. I have a friend whose core competency is not publishing but 'delivering ideas to clients.'

Deep down, what are your core competencies?

The Hedgehog
The fox, renowned for his cunning, has many strategies for killing the hedgehog. On the other

hand; the hedgehog has only one strategy for defending itself. Whenever the fox attacks, from whatever direction, the hedgehog rolls itself into a ball of spikes. It works every time. The hedgehog is supremely good at one thing, and it survives by sticking to its winning strategy. Identifying your own enterprise's Hedgehog Strategy flows from a thorough and objective understanding of what you can (and cannot) do and be world class at.

One of the reasons to assess your competitive strengths is to answer the question: What can your business be world class at? Note that the question is not what you would like to be world class at, but what you can be. Knowing this, and then playing ruthlessly to your key strength, is part of a successful Hedgehog Strategy.

The 95:5 Rule

The 95:5 Rule describes the way that an important few things are responsible for most of the impact on events. For example 95% of sales can come from 5% of products. 95% of profits can come from 5% of customers. Or 95% of your competitive advantage could be derived from just 5% of your strengths. (Also, 95% of headaches are caused by 5% of colleagues!) Etcetera...

When searching for opportunities and threats, the knack is to pick out the important few from the trivial many, because here, as elsewhere, the Pareto Principle applies. Based on economist Wilfredo Pareto's observation that 80% of the wealth was owned by 20% of the population in Italy at the time, the Pareto Principle is also known as the '80:20 Rule.' I find it's usually more of a 95:5 Rule.

Weaknesses may be plentiful and can be found in any area of the PSWA checklist. The good news is that they don't all need to be fixed. Playing to your strengths also includes playing away from your weaknesses. Your business formula includes deciding what not to do. Only weaknesses which could jeopardize your business strategy need to be rectified. See Chapter 8: On Your Route to Success.

Skills: Training or Learning?

There are many more ways of learning than attending training courses. As well as recognizing your enterprise's key skills (core competencies), there will be areas where skills need to be improved, and given the changing external environment and changing needs of customers, constant learning is inevitably an ingredient of success. A training needs analysis that can be undertaken to assess the gaps in skills and knowledge essential to the business strategy, though, personally, I prefer to focus on 'learning needs' rather than 'training needs'. Learning is much wider than training. A culture of encouraging learning is much more important than a budget for training.

Lifelong learning is not just a buzzword but a fact of life and a programme of Continuing Professional Development. This is essential for all individuals playing a part in the enterprise to ensure that their skills and knowledge are kept up to date for the benefit of the business and its customers. Each person could have a Personal Development Portfolio or plan.

The Learning Organization

At a corporate level, there needs to be a philosophy of building a Learning Organisation, which I describe as a company or other institution within which everybody continuously learns: from customers, from the competition and from colleagues. Just as important is a culture where this learning is shared with colleagues and through systems, this knowledge is embedded within the organisation as 'structural intellectual capital.' This is the knowhow in the firm which is more than the sum total of individuals' expertise and belongs to the organisation rather than (or as well as) the people working within it.

In a creative enterprise, constant learning and the buildup of knowledge should be part of a Business Dashboard and monitored as closely as financial measures of success. Crucially, the priorities for learning must be aligned to the overall business strategy, rather than individuals' personal preferences.

Key points:

1. Assess the strengths and weaknesses of yourself and your business, including all stakeholders.

2. Use the PSWA checklist.

3. Ask outsiders to help – they may see weaknesses and strengths you don't.

4. Remember that not all weaknesses need to be fixed.

5. Identify the core competencies at the root of your success.

6. Think of the hedgehog's strategy to find out what you can be world class at.

7. Use the 95:5 Rule to identify the most important 5% of your strengths and weaknesses.

8. Identify the additional learning and skills needs required to support the business strategy.

9. A culture of encouraging learning is much more important than a budget for training.

10. There are many more ways of learning than attending training courses. Think 'learning' rather than 'training' so as to open new possibilities for increasing knowledge and skills.

6
Business and Idea

- This chapter challenges the apparent contradiction between Creativity (ideas) and Business and suggests how they can be combined – creatively.

- It asks fundamental questions about why you are in a creative business or plan to be.

- It also discusses different approaches to business and the importance of being clear about your values and goals.

Creativity is not the monopoly of the artist - David Parish

Ideas vs. Business
Congratulations!
If you followed all the previous chapters and you took the exercises diligently, you should be ready for this chapter. I believe your mind must be set on your business now so let us examine what ideas mean to your product development and business. If creativity is getting new ideas and innovation is implementing it, let us share views on your business ideas and business itself.

Some people regard creativity and business as being like oil and water – they just don't mix. They think it's a question of choosing between creativity and business. I disagree.

At a conference I attended on the theme of creativity, some people understood creativity to mean 'art', done by artists of one kind or another. These artists realized that sometimes (unfortunately) they had to speak with beings from a parallel universe, i.e. the business world and inevitably didn't understand them. I reject the idea that business and creativity are incompatible opposites. At that conference I told them that I am a graphic artist, published writer and a business scholar, which perhaps unsettled a few people for a moment. I went on to say that my best creativity is not my graphic designs but my inventiveness within the business world, adapting ideas and methods to new circumstances across the boundaries of industries, sectors and cultures generally. Other delegates confirmed that they had seen far more creativity in engineering firms than in some advertising agencies. A creativity analyst, David Parish once said "Creativity is not the monopoly of the 'artist'": it is much wider than that and can be found in education, science and elsewhere. Creativity is in and around us all.

Creative Alchemy

The most exciting creativity, I believe, is the alchemy of blending apparent opposites, what we often call 'art' and 'science', recognizing that they are not opposites at all, from which we have to choose either/or in a binary fashion, but the yin and yang of a whole. This chapter is about bringing together creativity (ideas you have generated) and business as allies. It's about combining the best ideas of 'serious' creativity in the business of creativity, turning creative talent into income streams.

Successful creative entrepreneurs embrace both creativity and business. Perhaps, they don't use business jargon and maybe profit is not their primary aim. Sometimes, they will proceed on a hunch, or put their success down to good luck, but there is nevertheless a method behind their apparent madness, whether they recognize it or not.

The art of business is to select from a palette of infinite choices to draw together a specific product or service, with specific customers' needs, in a way that adds up financially. The resulting picture is a unique business formula for a successful enterprise.

Naturally, creative businesses tend to have a high concentration of new ideas in their product or service. Successful organisations of all kinds combine all the essential business elements creatively. Successful creative enterprises need to have a creative product or service; they also need to invent a special and workable formula which combines all the essential ingredients of business.

The 'Selling Out'
I am often asked whether making a creative business inevitably means compromising your fun integrity and be serious all the time or in other words, 'selling out.' My answer is that it can be, but it doesn't have to. The solution is in the formula mentioned above which refers to specific products/services and specific customers who, if chosen carefully, are essential ingredients in the formula for success. If you combine the wrong customers with your product

or service there will be a mismatch leading to a choice between selling out and going bust. You cannot sell all of your products to all your customers at all time, but if we apply some creativity to selecting the right customers, choosing appropriate products from our portfolio, whilst making the books balance at the same time, we can devise a feasible business formula.

Success
The meaning of 'success' is for you to define, not me. There are no value judgments here about what exactly 'success' might mean. Bigger is not necessarily better; often small is beautiful. You must decide where you want your creative enterprise to be in the future. As they say: "If you don't know where you want to be, then you will never figure out which road to take." So, your road to success depends on your destination – where you want to be in the future – your Vision.

Profit?
Profit is not always the point – though even not-for-profit organisations cannot survive if expenditure exceeds total income. As well as spanning subsectors, there are different economic models adopted in the creative and cultural industries sector: commercial businesses seeking profit, not-for-profit or charitable organizations and social enterprises. That's why I refer to 'the desired financial result' rather than necessarily 'making profit.' Many organisations are constituted as charities and their income includes grants and subsidies. Social enterprises define success with the Tripod stand approach, measuring success on three counts: financial, social and environmental. Some creative entrepreneurs are also 'social entrepreneurs.'

Lifestyle
'Lifestyle businesses' succeed by delivering both a healthy income and a rich quality of life for their owners. For others, success means building a profitable business that eventually doesn't need them, so, they can sell it and move on. And some

people want their creativity to sit alongside with another career as a hobby rather than a business.

Why do it?
For those wishing to embark on a journey into creative enterprise, the first question must be: Why do it? Why build a business around your passion? The obvious answer is to express your creativity and make a good living at the same time. But, is it that simple? This book outlines a range of challenges affecting businesses and offers some pointers towards solutions. There are many hurdles to overcome, compromises to be made and tough decisions to make along the way. So, first it's worth taking stock of what's at the heart of your creative enterprise and why you do it – or plan to do it.

Though, the intention is to allow your creativity 'free rein' by doing it fulltime as a business, some people complain that now that they are in business, they have less time for their creative passion, not more. Others have considered changing to a conventional job to earn money so as to be able to indulge their creativity in a pure way, free of the constraints and pressures of business.

Perhaps, it is better to separate earning a living on one hand and creativity on the other so as to do each one to the utmost, rather than doing neither one properly. Is there a risk that your creativity will be curbed by business? You may consider this suggestion inappropriate in a book like this, but, it is better to deal with this issue frankly now if it is a matter you may be facing – or likely to face in the future.

Yes, there is a risk of compromising your creativity with business and compromising your business profitability by indulging your creativity if you don't get the business formula right. For example, a financial formula that works for a hobby usually does not work for a business when higher prices need to be charged to cover the real costs of labour and other expenses.

Where?
Where do you want to be in the future? Pick a significant future date or milestone in your life (it doesn't have to be 'in five years' time,' though it could be). Describe what your business will look like. Who will be your clients? How many people will be involved? What level of income will you achieve? Draw up a blueprint for your goals. Be ambitious. Select a destination which is out of reach but not out of sight. This is your Vision.

What?
What business are you in? The best people to answer this are your customers. You might think you're in the website design business but your customers see you as their marketing consultant; you might describe yourself as a theatre company but what your customers are buying is a medium for communicating messages about social issues. Listen to customers to find out what they really value about you. What is the value to add for customers and your contribution to a better world? Answer the customer's question 'What's in it for me?' to find out what it is you really do for them. This is your Mission. You don't need to have a 'mission statement' (especially not a glib one), but you do need to understand what customers value about your business and what they really pay you for.

How?
How do you do business?, i.e. what are your beliefs, morals and ethics? Your Values. Sometimes these are so much a part of us we cannot see them, or just take them for granted. For example, my clients pointed out that my ability to listen, respect others' views and help them achieve their goals in their own way were my special values; but they were so much an integral part of me that I couldn't see them. I had missed the point and my publicity highlighted my professional qualifications instead. Ask other people: associates, friends, colleagues and especially customers in order to see yourself and your business more clearly. See Chapter 5: You and your idea

When?

Is the time right? Are you ready to go into business now or should you wait until a better time? A renowned photographer, Sharon Mutch left her photographic art under dust covers for nine years before setting up in business. When you have put together the answers to the Where, What, How and When questions, the next matter to consider is whether or not it all adds up into a workable business formula, a business model that's realistic and achievable.

Vision, Mission and Values

Vision: describes where we are going – the 'promised land.' The Vision is the enterprise's 'dream' of the future, a picture painted in words (and numbers) which is intended to inspire people by appealing to the heart as well as the head.

Mission: describes what we are going to do to achieve our Vision. A mission statement is simply a specific description of what the organization actually does – its contribution to the world and society – so that employees, customers and other stakeholders understand what the business needs to excel at.

Values: describe how we are going to conduct ourselves along the road to success.

Key points:

1. Some people think that creativity and business don't mix. I disagree. Think of business and creativity as partners, not opposites.

2. Some people understand creativity to mean 'art', done by artists of one kind or another.

3. Creative talent does not automatically 'deserve' business success. Not all creative ideas make feasible businesses.

4. Making a business out of creativity does not involve selling out - as long as you invent the right business formula.

5. As well as a creative product or service, you will need to create a unique and feasible business formula.

6. Be clear about your own definition of success. Know where you want to get to - your Vision.

7. Clarify your specific business Mission.

8. Recognize and hold on to your Values.

9. Decide whether now is the right time to start or expand.

7

Marketing Your Product

- This chapter explains that the real meaning of marketing is not about advertising and selling but choosing the right customers in the first place, then being prepared to put them at the centre and build your business around their requirements, listen to them and respond to their changing needs.

Launch the attack on as narrow a front as possible - Marketing Warfare

You are welcome to this chapter and I must say that it has been an intriguing journey so far. This chapter will reveal more about simple mistakes folks make about marketing comparing it to sales and advertising. If you can flow along with this chapter then, you have absolutely cleared the air of any impediment to your product marketing.

There is often great misunderstanding about marketing. People consider marketing to be the same as advertising. It's not. Advertising is only one part of marketing. Very simply put, marketing is the wide range of activities involved in making sure that you are continuing to meet the needs of your customers and getting value in return.

Marketing analysis includes finding out what groups of customers (or markets) exist, what their needs are, what groups of customers you prefer to serve (target markets), what products or services you might develop to meet their needs, how the customers prefer to use the products or services you might develop to meet their needs, what your competitors are doing, what pricing you should use and how you should distribute products and services to customers. Results of this marketing analysis indicate the position, or market "niche", for the organization to work from - and to be seen as having. Marketing also includes ongoing promotions, which can include advertising, public relations, sales and customer services. Various methods of market research are used to find out information about markets, target markets and their needs, competitors, market trends, customers satisfaction with products and services, etc.

One day, I was taking a class in Creative Entrepreneur - Program that involves creative marketing plans. One of the students asked me a question that really provoked me to think-through some marketing philosophies. I saw marketing as solving problems but this time, different convectional problems.

'Marketing' isn't just a posh word for 'selling.' It's much more radical than that. Marketing in its widest and best sense is about aligning your whole business to the changing needs of your customers.

An actor, Oscar Wilde wrote: "The play was a great success but the audience was a total failure." Some people tell me their business is fine – the problem is the customers! Usually a lack of them. The 'marketing problem' they claim to have is that they cannot convince people to buy their things. Their real problem is that their business is built around themselves and their products or services, not around customers' needs. They do their thing in a customer-free zone, a kind of creative vacuum. They are product-focused, not customer-focused.

Then, they hope that some marketing magic will sell it. It's as if they believe marketing is a kind of magic dust that clever marketers can sprinkle onto any old product or service to make it sell like hot cakes to anyone.

Successful creative enterprises are truly customers focused, not in the sense of putting customers in their sights (as if firing products at them), but putting the customer at the center of their universe so that their entire business revolves around them. It's a fundamentally different philosophy. It's a shift of thinking; from **How can we sell what we want to create?** to **How can we use our creativity to provide what customers want to buy?**

The word 'marketing' encompasses both science and art as well as a wide range of skills, but essentially, it can be separated into strategic marketing and operational marketing.

Strategic and Operational Marketing
Operational marketing is the more visible side: advertising, PR and selling that is about communicating towards customers, telling them

about products and services. Strategic marketing concerns itself with deciding what products and services to produce in the first place based on customers' changing needs. It is responsible for aligning the whole organization around the needs of particular customers. It's crucial that strategic marketing comes first because unless your initial business formula is right – matching particular products and services with selected customers profitably , then operational marketing will fail, no matter how clever (or creative) the advertising.

The strategic marketing formula includes decisions about which customers to serve. This is not a matter of opportunism but at the heart of your business formula and route to success in Chapter 8.

Customer Focus
Selecting the right customers in the first place is an essential element of any successful business formula. Then, organizing your enterprise around the changing needs of these selected clients or market segments is what marketing really means. In other words, putting customers first – at the beginning of the business process, not at the end. Customers' needs have to be the whole point of the business from beginning to end. That's why David Packard cofounder of Hewlett Packard famously said: "Marketing is too important to be left just to the marketing department." Marketing is the responsibility of the whole business, not just the sales people make at the end of the line.

The most strategically focused businesses have a list of target clients that they have identified as fitting in with their business strategy. David Ogilvy, founder of advertising agency Ogilvy and Mather wrote in his book Confessions of an Advertising Man how he built up his business by targeting clients and focused on getting their accounts at all costs. Ogilvy and Mather's client list over 50 years, includes names such as American Express, Ford, Shell, Barbie, Kodak, IBM, Dove and Maxwell House.

Marketing is definitely not a matter of trying to 'please all the customers all the time,' but selecting the customers you can partner with most effectively and profitably, matching their needs with your creative skills. Just as business strategy includes deciding what not to do, strategic marketing includes deciding which customers not to deal with. Not all customers are good customers. Trying to focus on every possible customer is not being focused at all!

Segmenting the Market
Market Segmentation is the process of dividing potential customers into groups with similar characteristics – perhaps geography, gender, age, needs, industry, or whatever is most useful or relevant. Analyzing customer segments allows clear decisions to be made about prioritizing target segments and deciding which types of customers to avoid because they do not fit the specification of your business formula. It can also help with **operational marketing** as each segment's similar characteristics can help to identify the most effective media channels to use to approach each group. One particularly useful way of segmenting customers is based on the media they read and watch, since this also automatically indicates which advertising media to use.

I once spent two and half hour meeting with a new client. In our discussion, I stopped her from making a terrible mistake that will set back her new product. I also led her to see how she can use her product to get the desired financial target. I told her to choose her customers and customize them. After a while, I received a call from her telling me how she had grown in a short while.

Existing customers are a useful resource, because analyzing their characteristics can help you understand which market segments you can work with best. Despite the strategic approach advocated here, your customer base may have developed more by accident than by design. And your current customers may help you to understand your business

strengths and weaknesses – if you ask them. Se
PSWA Checklist.

Furthermore, it's easier and cheaper (up to fiv
times as much, it is said) to win more businesse
from existing clients compared to winning nev
customers. Take care of them! In addition, existin
customers can be the route to new clients. Word c
mouth is the best advertising (and the cheapest) sc
encourage it to happen if it leads to the right kind c
customer.

Listening to Customers
I taught a course called Guerrilla Tactics – action
you can take every day without your boss'
permission. It is most suitable for employees on ho
to solve basic problems of the organisation an
dealing with customers alike. It would hel
organisations move forward by generating simpl
ideas that would keep her on track and help manag
customers effectively and productively. Man
organisations have given me feedback on how th
tips have been helpful. I can remember a particula
one that said, "We are no longer mindful c
competition, we keep moving and others kee
competing with us.

So if customers are the whole point of the business
from beginning to end, it's clearly not enough to tal
to them at the end, but to listen to them from th
beginning. Marketing is a dialogue, not a monologue
Listening to customers has many dimensions but it i
primarily an attitude towards customers as activ
partners, not passive targets. This involves looking a
things from the customers' point of view.

Marketing can be described as 'being close to th
customer' and it includes market research but no
only the stereotypical market research (which make
me think of avoiding eye contact with people sellin
materials at bus stops and those annoying unwante
phone calls from my network provider when I'm i
the middle of something important). There are man
ways of listening to customers and looking at thing
from the customers' point of view if you want to.

you really want to know about markets and customers, you can find out through various means, indirect and direct. As well as direct (primary) research, market research also includes secondary (desk) research using published data from industry analyses, government statistics and trade journals, much of which is available in libraries or on the Internet.

More directly you can visit customers, invite them to focus groups, and watch them use your product (or a competitor's). Visit them to see how they work. Get customers involved in new product development as new mind do. Explore how you can help their businesses develop. Last but not the least, listen to them and establish a dialogue through feedback mechanisms, focus groups, suggestions boxes (See Chapter One), or over a lunch. Buy them a drink and get to know them. In return, you'll get their good ideas and loyalty.

Sometimes insights emerge about what customers are really buying, which may not be what you think you are selling to them. For example, the apocryphal tales of the beer that was bought only because the empty can make an excellent oil lamp in Botswana; the bookstore that found nobody returned the voucher placed deep inside the Booker Prize winning novel because in reality people bought it to leave on their coffee table to impress their friends. Such unsettling observations help you to see things from the customer's point of view.

Ask yourself: What do you know about your current customers, lost customers and target customers? What would you like to know? Devise a way of finding out.

Operational Marketing
If you get your strategic marketing right, then, operational marketing becomes much easier. In other words, if you have devised a business formula around a natural fit between selected customers and the products they want, at the right price, then advertising and promotion becomes more a matter

of informing them rather than coercing them. There's no need for cold calling or hard selling if you've listened to customers all along and they've been included in the project from the start. On the other hand, even the most persuasive (or 'creative') advertising will not sell a product if it's not what the customers want and at the right price.

Let me say something about our convectional Ps of marketing. I know many would not come to terms with this chapter if I fail to mix the four Ps of marketing with my own analysis. The Marketing Mix is a blend of the Four Ps of Marketing: Product, Price, Promotion and Place. (Place really means Distribution but '3 Ps and a D' doesn't have the same ring to it.) These four controllable and convectional elements can be blended in different ways to maximize sales – so long as the product is right for the carefully selected target market.

Promotion is actually just one aspect of the marketing mix but it's what people often mean when they use the term 'marketing' as shorthand for advertising, public relations (PR) or other channels of marketing communications including direct mail and attending trade shows. All of these are essentially about getting the right message to the right people in the most effective way, emphasizing benefits not features.

Operational marketing is always limited by budgets and that budget can be very small indeed, especially for new creative businesses. Sometimes, however, the cheapest is the best – word of mouth recommendations for example – so, encourage this to happen and reward it when it does. Some organisations give a percentage commission for recommendations that lead to new work. Viral Marketing, used extremely effectively by Hotmail to advertise itself at the bottom of messages as emails zoom around the Internet is also used by Online Originals as their ebooks are sent between friends sharing works of literature.

By adopting an attitude to customers as partners rather than passive targets, interactive forms of marketing come to mind. For example, websites that people can engage with (not just read) and printed materials that invite a response all treat customers as active participants.

Rather than thinking of expensive and relatively untargeted mass marketing (which in any case would be inappropriate for most creative businesses) turn this approach on its head and decide which single customer would be perfect if you could only have one. Then, track down this ideal customer, then find one more, then another and so on.

In conclusion, marketing is not a magic dust that can make anything sell. The magic of marketing works when you put customers at the center and build your enterprise around their needs. Customers! Please remember that word.

Key Points

1. Marketing is not just a posh word for selling. It's much more radical than that.

2. Sort out your strategic marketing (part of your business formula) before planning your operational marketing.

3. Target specific market segments or specific customers. Draw up a target list of clients to win.

4. Marketing is a dialogue, not a monologue. It includes listening to customers as well as talking to them.

5. Not all customers are good customers. Decide which are good and bad for your enterprise.

6. Are you customer focused or product focused?

7. Build your business around customers' changing needs. Be prepared to change as customers' needs do.

8. How much do you know about your current customers, lost customers and target customers? What would you like to know? Devise a way of finding out what you need to know, through various means including direct and indirect market research.

9. Help and encourage existing customers to recommend you to new customers – so long as they are the right kind.

8

Route to Success

This chapter is concerned with pulling together all the elements considered so far and formulating a specific plan for your feasible creative business.

I should have talked about this part from the beginning but I cannot motivate you on an empty platform. I must be certain that you have gotten the right content before switching to some motivational summary of all I have written.

To be successful in business is tasking but achievable. To do it again is even more tasking but also achievable. I will leave you with few pieces of advice.

First, you need to be clear about the success you want to achieve – your Vision.

Then, you need a realistic plan to get there – your Business Strategy or route to success. This route must be based on your unique business formula.

A business formula is your unique mixture of particular products/services at which you excel, carefully selected customers or market segments which can combine to produce the desired financial result, consistent with your Values.

A feasible business formula must be based on realistic assessment of the market, competitors and a SWOT Analysis of your own Strengths and Weaknesses, combined with opportunities and threats in the changing world.

Clearly, you will play to your strengths, seize opportunities, fully understand selected customers needs and position yourself shrewdly among competitors.

Here are seven steps to help you on your journey to successful business
It all boils down to seven steps:

1. Be clear where you want to go – your Vision.
2. Know yourself and your current situation.
3. Understand customers' needs, competition and external forces.
4. Carefully create your unique business formula.

5. Devise a plan of action – your Business Strategy.
6. Turn the plan into action.
7. Stick to it – be prepared to Say No.

Of course, there will be thousands of things to do along the way (tasks) and some important decisions to be made (tactics) but the strategy is about the big issues – the essential milestones or key turning points along the way. It is impossible to plan precisely the exact and detailed series of tasks, or predict the tactics you will have to use, but there will be several essential big steps to be taken. These will be different for each enterprise but they might include vital matters such as finding an international partner, investing in new technology, protecting and exploiting intellectual property, attracting investment, etc.

A creative way to think about this is to imagine you are in the future and have achieved your success. In an interview, telling the story of your journey, you look back on the key decisions and actions that proved to be turning points or vital ingredients of your success. Perhaps, there were four or five critical moves that you will look back on from the future. Returning to the present, you now have a list of the key things you need to do.

Note that this applies equally to not-for-profit organisations as well as commercial businesses and can be applied to personal as well as organisational goals.

Implementing a strategy is not always easy to plan since you cannot predict just how and when particular opportunities will arise or circumstances will change, but if you know what you are looking for, you can look in the right direction or spot opportunities if they come your way.

A vital ingredient of implementing the plan is sticking to it and that means Saying 'No' to opportunities that are not in line with your business formula and strategic plan.

Measuring Performance

Along the way, you will need to monitor progress in different ways: firstly, to make sure you are not deviating substantially from your business formula and are right on track to hit the key milestones; secondly, to make sure that your business is progressing at the right pace. Deciding what needs to improve, and what doesn't, is an integral part of a clear business strategy.

You can then set targets for improving the important things and these can be called Key Performance Indicators (KPIs). Depending on your business, they might include targets for sales, customer satisfaction, profitability, innovation, growth, market penetration, developing core skills, etc.

Using the balanced scorecard approach, these should include financial measures but not exclusively. A business dashboard for your own enterprise should also take into account customers, creativity, learning and efficiency. This provides you with a business dashboard or control panel which constantly shows how things are developing and quickly brings to your attention anything that isn't going well so that you can take appropriate action immediately.

Imagine you are away from the business for a year, but want to know how things are going. What ten pieces of information would you want to receive on a single piece of paper each week to give you an overview of the business? The answer to this is your specification for designing your own business dashboard.

Depending on your philosophies and priorities, you may want to measure success using the Tripod stand approach, measuring financial performance, social benefits and the environmental impact of your business. This is a way that social enterprises measure success and is increasingly being adopted by large corporations who are eager to demonstrate that their motivations are not purely financial.

Risks

Risks are part of any business and calculated risks will have to be taken, based on a risk Analysis. You will probably face a range of financial and legal risks as well as risks to your brand and personal wellbeing.

Risk Analysis is simply the technique of listing all risks and ranking them according to their likelihood of happenings and the potential negative impact on the business. The point, of course, is to minimize the risks, focusing first on those risks that score high on both counts and making plans to make them less likely to happen or having a lesser impact if they do. A calculated assessment of risks is an important element of choosing the best route to success. An action plan to deal with risks will help to navigate that chosen route without mishaps.

Business Plans

A detailed business plan is usually required to explain your intentions to investors and partners. Just as importantly, it should provide a useful guide for internal use by the owners/directors and staff. Some people find that writing a business plan is a nightmare. Others find that the exercise produces a useless document. In both cases, the reason is often that the proposed business is not based on the solid foundations of a feasible business formula.

It's essential to establish the fundamentals of **why** you are planning to do it as well as **how** you are planning to do it. Once you are clear about these matters and have the framework of a feasible formula which brings together your skills and your selected customers' needs in a financially sustainable way, then, the route to success becomes clear and the rest of the business plan will fall into place relatively easily.

There is no standard template for a business plan. In fact, you don't even have to call it a business plan –

Some organisation even preferred the term development Plan. It is simply your way of setting out your plans for yourself and for others in a comprehensive, clear and useful way. It should answer all the questions that a potential partner o investor might ask.

The best business plans are those that a creative entrepreneur actually wants to refer to often and is updated on a rolling basis as time goes by and circumstances change. Your business plan describes your route to success. It is your pocket guide on an exciting journey that helps you keep going in the right direction as the adventure unfolds.

- The Beginning -

www.ingramcontent.com/pod-product-compliance
Lightning Source LLC
Chambersburg PA
CBHW031533210526
45464CB00014B/2143